T0129062

Joseph "Joe Dogs" Iannuzzi

THE
MAFIA

COOKBOOK

Revised and Expanded

With 37 New, Foolproof
Recipes to Die For

SIMON & SCHUSTER

NEW YORK LONDON TORONTO SYDNEY TOKYO

SIMON & SCHUSTER
Rockefeller Center
1230 Avenue of the Americas
New York, NY 10020

The stories in the book are based on real events. In
some instances, dates, names, places, and other
details were changed to accommodate my recipes.–J.I.

For information about special discounts for bulk purchases,
please contact Simon & Schuster Special Sales:
1-800-456-6798 or business@simonandschuster.com

Designed by Barbara Marks

Manufactured in the United States of America

9   10   8

Library of Congress Cataloging-in-Publication Data
Iannuzzi, Joseph.
The Mafia cookbook / Joseph "Joe Dogs" Iannuzzi.
p.   cm.
1. Cookery, Italian.   2. Cookery, International.
3. Mafia—United States.   I. Title.
TX723 .I42 2001
641.5945—dc21   2001049582
ISBN 978-1-4767-4348-6

For my children:

Sheryl

Debra

Stephanie

Sonja

Joseph III

THIS BOOK IS DEDICATED TO MY
GOOD FRIEND AND *COMPARE* TOMMY AGRO—
WITHOUT YOU, THIS BOOK WOULD NOT BE POSSIBLE.
REST IN PIECES.

THANK YOU, MARILYN RITZ,
FOR WALKING INTO THE KITCHEN OF
DON'S ITALIAN RESTAURANT
ON SINGER ISLAND, FLORIDA, ON
JANUARY 19, 1981, AND SAVING MY LIFE.
THANKS A MILLION.

—*JOE DOGS*

The Mafia Cookbook

Recipes

More recipes may be found in "Cooking on the Lam," page 159.

Introduction

I like to cook. I've always liked to cook. That is, as long as I didn't have to cook, I liked it. It was when I was made to cook that I hated it, because if I didn't do it they'd either fire me or, later, fire *at* me.

I learned the hard way. How to cook, that is. When I was a kid my stepfather kicked me out of the house. He was an Irish bastard. So I had to learn quick. You follow me? I think I was thirty-eight or thirty-nine years old when that Irish ____ told me to cop a walk. Just kidding. I was fifteen years old. So I bounced around the pool halls until I was old enough to join the army. I was a GFU (General Flake-Up), so I was constantly on KP. The mess sergeant went out of his way to show me different recipes to cook and bake. Not because he was such a nice and generous guy. Because he was a fat, lazy SOB who wanted me to learn so he could laze around on his fat ass all day.

After the army I got married and divorced and married and divorced and, in the early fifties, somehow found myself in Cleveland, Ohio. I needed a job, so I applied for work in one of the classiest restaurants in Cleveland. The chef who interviewed me laughed like hell when I told him my references and experiences. "Joey," the chef said, "if you promise me to forget everything you've learned about cooking I'll give you a job." *Voilà!* I was in. The kitchen. As a saucier.

I learned how to make soups and sauces, and I experimented

cooking with brandies and different wines. After six months I figured I had the experience to cook anywhere, even the Big Apple, my hometown. So I stole another car and drove back to New York. (I couldn't very well drive the stolen car that had taken me to Ohio back to New York.) Back in New York: another marriage, another divorce. Oh-for-three.

Anyway, I worked in different diners and restaurants around New York, cooking food and making book. Through my bookmaking partners I got an application to join a very exclusive club: the Mothers And Fathers Italian Association—MAFIA, for short. Normally you needed a college degree to be accepted, as there were some very intelligent guys in this club. Some could *almost* read and write. But they let me slide into their club because of my cooking. They said they would "learn" me the rules and regulations as time went on.

Now, mobsters love to eat. They eat while planning crimes and they eat after committing crimes, and when there are no crimes, they eat while waiting for them to happen. And mobsters are very picky. They know what they like, and when they like it they eat all of it. And then more. Look at the stomachs on these guys the next time television shows one of them being escorted into court in handcuffs. These are some very serious eaters.

Which is why some of these recipes call for such heavy sauces. Remember the crowd I was feeding—any meal may be their last, so it better be a good one. Crime may not pay, but it sure gives you a hell of an appetite.

So don't be scared off by the butter and cream. Just serve the richer sauces on the side instead of dumping them on top of the food.

My cooking for my mentor, my rabbi, my *compare*, Tommy

Agro, came in very handy, as "T.A." was constantly on the lam. Tommy A. and his crew were forever traveling to different apartments in different states to lay low, and we'd always leave in a rush and I wouldn't even get to pack up my pots and pans and knives. "Leave them, Joey" was T.A.'s familiar refrain. "We'll buy new ones." Despite these culinary hardships, lamming it was a good experience. I was perfecting my craft.

The members of my new club ate a lot of veal and an awful lot of pasta. But that didn't stop me from experimenting with dishes. I'd never tell the crew what I was cooking if it wasn't a recipe from the old country. They wouldn't have eaten it (and they might have shot me). But once they were licking their chops, I'd let them in on the fact that they were wolfing down Mandarin Pork Roast, or Steak au Poivre, and I never received a complaint.

I cooked for the club—among other jobs—for about ten years. Then I had a terrible accident. I kept walking into this baseball bat and this iron pipe. Some of my pals were trying to see if my head was harder than those two instruments. It was, just barely. But because of this experience I was enticed to join another club on a sort of double-secret probation. This club was called the Full-Blooded Italians, or FBI, for short. The guys in my new club asked me to spy on the guys in my old club who had tried to kill me. I had no problem with that. Revenge, like my Cicoria Insalata, is best eaten cold.

When it came to food, the members of my new club were no different from the members of my old club. They all ate like they were going to the chair. You don't have to eat that way with the recipes in this book. You just have to enjoy them. Because they've been tested on the worst of the worst and the best of the best. And they've all passed with flying colors.

Menu

Pasta Marinara
Veal Marsala

HALLANDALE, FLORIDA, 1974
TOMMY AGRO'S APARTMENT

PEOPLE PRESENT:
Joe Dogs
Tommy "T.A." Agro (Gambino soldier)
Louie Esposito
Skinny Bobby DeSimone
Buzzy Faldo (Gambino Associates; T.A.'s Florida crew)

*T*ommy Agro was down from New York, on the lam from an extortion bit handed up by a federal grand jury. I didn't find out how my *compares* always learned ahead of time about these so-called secret indictments until years later. Turns out they'd planted a mole in the U.S. Attorney's office, a secretary who typed up the paperwork, handed it to her boss, and immediately called the Gambinos with a warning.

Anyway, Tommy (aka T.A.) had blown town in a hurry, and he was nervous. And when T.A.—moody on a good day—was nervous, I liked to stay traditional. It only upset him more when I experimented in the kitchen. So veal and pasta were just the trick. Tommy sat down to a pinochle game with some of our south Florida Gambino crew—Louie Esposito, Skinny Bobby DeSimone, and Buzzy Faldo—while I headed for the stove to whip up a pot of my special marinara sauce. This is a classic. Just throw in a littl'a this, a littl'a that and you got a sauce to die for (you should pardon the expression).

Pasta Marinara

MARINARA SAUCE

2 cloves garlic, crushed and chopped fine
¼ cup olive oil (extra-virgin or virgin preferred)

1 (28-ounce) can peeled tomatoes (Progresso Pomodori
Pelati con Basilico or Pope brand preferred),
chopped fine
½ teaspoon garlic powder
¼ teaspoon dry mustard
¼ teaspoon pepper
2 tablespoons crushed dried basil
1 cup chicken stock

*I*n a small saucepan sauté garlic in olive oil until garlic dissolves (do not brown or burn). Add chopped tomatoes, stir, and simmer for 5 minutes. Add remaining ingredients, stir, and allow to simmer over low heat for approximately 25 to 30 minutes. Serve over your favorite pasta.

"Hey Joey," Tommy yelled from the living room while the sauce was simmering. "You didn't tell your wife that I'm here, did you? I don't want anybody to know I'm down here."

"Damn, Tommy, I wish you would have told me this before," I answered. Of course I hadn't told Bunny, but it was time to get Tommy's goat a little, loosen him up. "I already told her. In fact, I heard her telling her girlfriend Margie about you."

"Who the hell is Margie?" T.A. exploded. "Can't you guys do anything without reporting to your _____ing wives?"

"Oh, Margie, she's the girl who's married to the Florida State's Attorney," I answered. "I'm sure she'll tell her husband about you. She knows you're a Mafia guy."

"Joey, you get back in that kitchen before I eat your _____ing eyes for dinner."

Okay, Tom, the blue-plate eyeball special for you—everyone else gets the veal.

~~~~~

Veal Marsala

½ cup flour
1½ pounds veal (scaloppini cut), pounded thin with
    mallet
6 ounces (1½ sticks) butter, melted (clarified preferred)
¾ cup Florio sweet Marsala wine
2 ounces Grand Marnier
1 pound mushrooms, cleaned, sliced, and sautéed
    (see Note)
Juice of ½ lemon
¼ teaspoon white pepper

Flour veal on both sides. Heat butter in frying pan (do not burn). Shake off excess flour and sauté veal on both sides, lightly, over medium to low heat. Remove veal and set aside. Pour wine into saucepan and stir. Then add Grand Marnier, stir, and ignite to burn off alcohol. After flame dies, cook sauce until condensed to half the amount, put veal back in saucepan, and cook for another 5 minutes, stirring occasionally. Stir in the sautéed mushrooms, lemon juice and pepper and serve. *Serves 4 to 6.*

Note: To sauté mushrooms, clean and slice them and sauté them in ¼ pound melted butter. Add 2 ounces sweet sherry and cook over low flame for 20 minutes, stirring occasionally.

～

"Joey, Joey, how do you get the sauce so sweet?" Skinny Bobby wanted to know.

"The Grand Marnier does it," I told him. "I burn out all the alcohol, though."

I sat back and watched everyone eat. They were gobbling up the food like it was their last meal. You would have thought they were all going to the chair. After dinner they all leaned back and made vulgar noises while I went to the kitchen to put coffee on.

"What the hell is this," I screamed, running out of the kitchen with a jar of pickles. Inside, nestled among the gherkins, was a human index finger. I threw it on the table and everyone started laughing.

"Oh, that's Frankie's finger," Tommy Agro said at last. "He used to tend bar for me. Whenever I open up a new joint I put that jar behind the bar, where all the people who work for me can see it. Then I put up a small sign that says, *This is Frankie's finger. It's here because he stole from his boss.* That way, any _____ who works for me will think twice before stealing. If I catch him a second time, they lose their hand. So far I got only one of those. It's home in my freezer in New York. Want me to bring it down next time I come, Joey?"

"*Marrone,* no!" I shook my head, and edged back into T.A.'s kitchen, on the lookout for any more body parts.

Menu

Monkfish Marinelli

HALLANDALE, FLORIDA, 1976
TOMMY AGRO'S APARTMENT

PEOPLE PRESENT:
Joe Dogs
Tommy Agro

I named this recipe in honor of a Colombo crime family soldier who used to pull B&Es with me up in Connecticut. He was also a big fisherman, and taught me how to fillet a fish. I usually only prepared this dish at home for me and my wife, Bunny. But when Tommy Agro called about a week after he'd hit town—still laying low in Florida—I decided to get a little daring. By this time he'd calmed down a little, so when he ordered me to get over to his apartment to cook dinner and discuss a race we were planning to fix at Gulfstream Park, I stopped by a dockside fishmonger on the way and picked up a fresh monkfish.

Monkfish Marinelli

¾ pound monkfish fillet

2 tablespoons olive oil (extra-virgin or virgin preferred)

⅓ cup flour

1 heaping tablespoon finely chopped garlic

¼ cup dry white wine

¼ pound (1 stick) butter

¼ cup chopped fresh parsley

Salt and pepper to taste

1 pound linguine

Cut monkfish into ½-inch-thick medallions. Heat olive oil in skillet. Dredge monkfish in flour (shake off excess). Sauté fish on both sides until golden brown. Stir in chopped garlic, add white wine, and simmer 5 minutes.

⌇⌇⌇

"So what's the chances of us getting double-banged on this race fix?" T.A. asked. He was nosing around the kitchen—bothering me—because there was no one else in the apartment to play pinochle with.

I explained to him for what must have been the hundredth time how I'd "reached" a crooked horse trainer named Sean O'Leary. Sean was a degenerate gambler, and he was into his shylock for close to 20 large. Unbeknownst to Sean, his shylock was in my crew. Anyway, Sean said that for around $15,000 in expense money up front he could get to four of the seven jocks in Saturday's sixth race at Gulfstream. That meant we only had to "wheel" the remaining three horses—all longshots—for a guar-

anteed winner. The split would be four ways: Me, T.A., Sean, and a Palm Beach bookmaker named Freddie Campo who I'd brought in to help me place the bets. In those days, the Florida tracks weren't computerized, and getting down, say, a $30,000 box at a betting window took a long time.

T.A. was satisfied with the setup, and pestered me to hurry up and finish cooking. Hey, Tommy, hold ya horses, will ya? I started the sauce to shut him up.

*A*dd butter to the simmering monkfish a little at a time. Then add chopped parsley, plus salt and pepper to taste. Cook pasta in 2 quarts salted water until *al dente*. Drain and place on platter, or individual plates. Place monkfish on pasta, and pour sauce from skillet over fish and pasta. *Serves 2.*

That Saturday the fix went down like a three-dollar fighter. Sean reached the jocks, who pulled the four favorites. Freddie Campo and I bet with both hands, each getting $15,000 down on longshot boxes. We took home $128,000. Subtracting the $30,000 we'd bet, and the $15,000 in "expenses," we'd cleared 83 large. Before the Gulfstream meet was over, our "consortium" had "won" approximately $800,000. I didn't know what I liked better, being a crook or being a cook.

Menu

Cicoria Insalata
(Dandelion Greens Salad)
Panacotte (Greens and Beans)

BROOKLYN, NEW YORK, 1975
LITTLE DOM CATALDO'S SAFE HOUSE

PEOPLE PRESENT:
Joe Dogs
Dominick "Little Dom" Cataldo (Colombo soldier and hitman)
Frank and Lino (Colombo associates, members of Little Dom's crew)

wo hours earlier, Little Dom Cataldo and I had been scrunched down in the front seat of his car, waiting for the carrier to come out of the loan office with the satchel. Little Dom was a soldier, and hitman, in the Colombo family. To look at him you'd never believe that the guy had murdered over ten people.

"I put him in Boot Hill" was one of Little Dom's favorite expressions. It wasn't brag. Just fact. Little Dom, who had a passing resemblance to the actor John Garfield, did have his own private burial grounds. A certain hill along the Taconic Parkway twenty miles or so north of New York City. But we hadn't capped anybody tonight. This had been a straight boost, $143,000 in drug money. The beauty part was, we'd ripped off another wiseguy whose capo had banned drug dealing. So who was the guy going to run to? Talk about your "no-fault" robberies.

Anyway, now we were back in Little Dom's safe house in Red Hook, Brooklyn, by the docks, divvying up the cash. It was me, Little Dom, and two of his crew, Frank and Lino. Everybody was hungry. Little Dom had told me he was tired of the "same old garbage." His heart was still racing, like it did whenever he nailed a big score, and he didn't want no meat. No problem. I decided on something light—a fresh salad with a nice vinaigrette and a vegetable casserole. As usual, his kitchen was stocked. The only thing I had to do was send Lino out for the dandelion greens.

Cicoria Insalata

1 bunch dandelion greens
½ cup olive oil (extra-virgin or virgin preferred)
1 teaspoon chopped garlic
1 tablespoon red wine vinegar (or lemon juice)
1 small red onion, sliced thin

*W*ash greens and pat dry. Add remaining ingredients to greens and toss thoroughly. Adjust seasoning to taste. *Serves 4.*

Panacotte (Greens and Beans)

1 head escarole
4 whole cloves garlic
2 tablespoons olive oil (extra-virgin or virgin preferred)
½ teaspoon crushed red pepper flakes (optional)
1 (16-ounce) can cannellini beans with juice (or approximately 1 cup dried beans, presoaked and cooked)
Salt and pepper to taste
2 cups cubed stale bread
½ cup freshly grated Parmesan cheese

*W*ash and tear escarole. Slowly sauté garlic cloves (whole) in olive oil. Remove frying pan from heat.

Allow to cool slightly. Add crushed red pepper and escarole and cook approximately 15 minutes over medium heat until tender. Add beans with juice and bring to boil. Taste for seasoning and add salt and pepper if needed. Put bread cubes in casserole dish with ¼ cup Parmesan cheese and escarole-and-bean mixture. Sprinkle remaining grated Parmesan (¼ cup) over top.

Bake in preheated 375-degree oven until slightly browned (approximately 20 minutes). Serve with crusty Italian bread, or Italian garlic bread, and wine. *Serves 4.*

⁓

"Joey, did I ever tell you about the time I popped that big fat Lucchese family guy?" Little Dom asked between delicious bites. "I hated this _____, he owed me vig for a long time, and I talked his own right-hand man, Johnny was his name, into conning him into meeting me in a parking lot in Queens.

"Anyway, after I whacked him, Johnny says to me, 'What're we gonna do with this fat pig now?' And since he got the guy there for me to whack, it's only fair I help him get rid of the body. So we stuff him into my trunk and drive to Boot Hill. I told Johnny that we gotta dig deep, five or six feet, 'cause the lime I use to cover the body smells, even through the ground. When we were finished, I drove my car as close as I could to the hole, and we threw the fat man in.

"Then I said, 'Damn, Johnny, I forgot to take his watch off, his ring and his dough. No sense in burying them.' So Johnny jumps in the hole to get the stuff and I shot him too. I put the lime in, then the dirt, then the grass seed. But I had a lot of dirt to spread around, because I had a two-story job there.

"Ha ha, that's funny, Joey. A two-story job."

Little Dom Cataldo cracked himself up.

Menu

Shrimp Scampi

North Miami Beach, Florida, 1974
Jiggs Forlano's Apartment

People Present:
Joe Dogs
Tommy Agro
Jiggs Forlano (Colombo capo)
Bobby "Bobby Anthony" Amelio and Rabbit Fusco (drug dealers)

*J*iggs was a Colombo family capo from Brooklyn who liked to tell people he'd retired to Miami. Yeah. You retire from the mob when you retire from the living. It's like the IRA motto: "Once in, never out." Anyway, Jiggs had set up a meet with two suitcases from New York who needed investors in a marijuana-smuggling operation. He figured Tommy Agro could come with some fast cash. T.A. brought me to the meet as backup.

Bobby Amelio (aka Bobby Anthony) and his partner, Rabbit Fusco, were a couple of knockaround Mafia wannabes—babes in the woods, we called those kind—who were always on the fringe of a hustle. T.A. didn't like them, but "like" didn't matter to Tommy when money was involved. Jiggs made the introductions and began pouring drinks while I headed for the kitchen to impress the guys with my Shrimp Scampi. Now I know you're gonna say, Whoa, half a pound of butter and sour cream?! But remember, these guys ain't exactly concerned about their cholesterol count. So when serving guests with more normal appetites just keep the sauce on the side.

Shrimp Scampi

2 pounds jumbo shrimp (preferably under 15 to a
   pound)
½ pound (2 sticks) butter
1 shallot, chopped fine
3 cloves garlic, crushed and chopped fine
2 cups sour cream

....

2 tablespoons chopped dried chives
1 teaspoon garlic powder
¼ teaspoon white pepper
1 teaspoon Accent (optional)

$\mathcal{S}$ hell, devein, and butterfly shrimp. Set on large flat pan or large microwave dish. Set aside.

"What are you gonna cook for these guys, Joe? I didn't know you knew how to cook." Jiggs, a huge man with an Italian cigar nub apparently surgically attached to the side of his mouth, looked impressed.

"I used to be a sauce chef when I was a working stiff," I told him. "I like foolin' around in the kitchen."

"You mean you retired from workin' so you could become T.A.'s valet, chauffeur, and _____ing cook?" he asked. I lifted a large carving knife and Jiggs went back out to the living room while I went back to my shrimp.

$\mathcal{M}$ elt butter in a good, thick metal pot (do not scorch). Add chopped shallot and garlic, and sauté for 3 to 5 minutes over low heat. Add sour cream and stir. (It is thick at first, but once heated it will thin.) Add chives, garlic powder, pepper, and Accent, if using. Simmer over low heat, stirring occasionally, for approximately 30 to 45 minutes until it thickens to a nice texture.

"Jiggs, you staying for dinner?" I shouted.

"I'd like to, Joey, but you guys got business to attend to what I don't want to know about. I'm gonna take a walk."

*T*f you're going to broil the shrimp, watch them closely so they don't overcook. If you microwave them, do so for 3 to 3½ minutes on high setting. Pour sauce over shrimp and serve with rice. *Serves 4.*

"Joey, I never had shrimp scampi like this before," Rabbit Fusco said.

"Me either," Bobby Anthony agreed, licking his chops. "Now listen, we got a ton of that stuff coming in on the boat from Colombia. It'll be here in about ten days. I need some front money from you guys."

"How much do we have to come up with?" I asked.

"Fifteen grand."

"*Marrone,*" T.A. whooshed. "And suppose I just hand youse this fifteen large? What's in it for me? I wasn't made with a finger, you know."

Baked Pork Chops
Philadelphia

WEST PALM BEACH, FLORIDA, 1975
MY HOME

PEOPLE PRESENT:
Joe Dogs
Tommy Agro

I invited Tommy Agro over to my house for dinner. I gave my wife, Bunny, who was also a good cook, the night off. Since the reefer smuggler Bobby Anthony (see Shrimp Scampi) never consummated his dope deal, Tommy shylocked out as a loan the $15,000 we had given him for the dope. But he'd been slow coming back with his payments. That extortion bit T.A.'d been dodging in New York looked like it was finally going to catch up with him, and he wanted to make contingency plans in case he had to go into the joint. This recipe is a man's-man kind of dinner I'd picked up from a Philly mobster vacationing in Miami, and I wanted to make this a special occasion, like a last meal, just in case I didn't see T.A. for a while.

Baked Pork Chops Philadelphia

2 tablespoons vegetable oil
4 pork chops (1 inch thick)
4 tablespoons (½ stick) butter
1 pound mushrooms, cleaned and sliced
2 shallots, grated or chopped very fine
Salt and pepper to taste
¼ cup cognac
¼ cup dry white wine
1½ tablespoons green peppercorns
1¼ cups heavy cream
1 tablespoon Accent (optional)

*H*eat vegetable oil in a fairly large saucepan. When hot, cook the pork chops for 3 minutes on each side to brown a little. Put pork aside. Add butter to pan and cook mushrooms and shallots for another 5 minutes. Season with salt and pepper. Then add cognac and wine and cook for another 4 minutes, stirring, over high heat. Mix peppercorns and cream in separate bowl. Crush peppercorns into cream. Add Accent. Pour mixture over mushrooms and shallots and simmer for 1 to 2 minutes, stirring occasionally.

⌒⌇⌒

From my living room, I heard the apoplectic T.A. yelling into the kitchen: "You tell this _____ Bobby Anthony that I want my _____ing money back. All of it. By no later than the first of the month. And I want a ten-grand bonus. You hear?"

⌒⌇⌒

*P*lace the pork chops in a baking pan. Pour the mushroom-shallot mixture over the pork. Cover and bake for 20 minutes in a preheated 350-degree oven. Serve with vegetable, potato, and applesauce.

⌒⌇⌒

"Joey, if I hafta go in and this guy don't deliver, I don't want you to do nothin'. I'll take care of this from the inside. I'll reach out for him. I need you out here watching my back. *Marrone,* what is this, Joey, pork? This is good. Ain't this what the Jews eat?"

"No, Tommy," I said. "Jewish people don't eat pork."

Menu

Mandarin Pork Roast
Rice and Ricotta Pudding

QUEENS, NEW YORK, 1976
UNDISCLOSED LOCATION

PEOPLE PRESENT:
Joe Dogs
Thomas DiBella (Boss, Colombo family)
Allie LaMonte (Colombo capo)
Dominick "Little Dom" Cataldo
assorted Colombo capos, soldiers, and associates

*T*alk about a dangerous meal. Cooking for capos had always been nerve-racking enough. But Thomas DiBella had just been named acting head of the Colombo crime family while Carmine "Snake" Persico did a stretch in the federal pen. The Colombo *famiglia* were fêting the new boss with a round of dinners. When Little Dominick Cataldo's turn rolled around, he flew me up from Florida to put on the dog. (Ooh, I love a bad joke.) Little Dom owned a club in Queens—and he gave me free run of the kitchen.

Little Dom was nervous. He wanted everything to be just right. There were more than a dozen Colombo crew members present, each of them a heavyweight. "Please make everything perfect for the new Scoutmaster," Dom begged me. "And, Joey, please watch your mouth tonight. I know how you're always calling us wops, and I understand it's a joke. But please don't let none of those old zips hear you talkin' like that."

I promised to behave myself, and got to work on the pork.

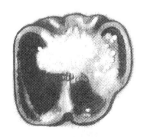

Mandarin Pork Roast

1 (6-pound) boneless pork loin (tied with string)
1 teaspoon salt
½ teaspoon white pepper
¾ teaspoon garlic powder
2¼ tablespoons Dijon mustard
1 (11-ounce) can mandarin oranges
¼ cup light brown sugar
¼ cup red wine vinegar
1 chicken bouillon cube
1¼ tablespoons soy sauce (low-salt)
2 tablespoons cornstarch
¾ cup water
1 medium onion, chopped
½ cup chopped green pepper

*T*rim excess fat from pork. Rub salt, pepper, and garlic powder into pork. Spread mustard over roast. Place roast in large dutch oven. Cover and bake in preheated 325-degree oven until meat thermometer reads 170 degrees (approximately 3 hours).

Drain oranges. Save liquid. Place orange liquid, brown sugar, vinegar, chicken bouillon cube, soy sauce, cornstarch, and water in saucepan. Cook, stirring, over medium heat until smooth and thickened. Remove from heat and stir in onion, green pepper, and oranges. Spoon sauce over roast and bake uncovered for 30 to 40 minutes, basting occasionally. Slice pork and serve with sauce. *Serves 14 to 16.*

I was allowed to dine with the Colombo boss and his soldiers—the only Gambino honored like that at the table. After dinner, DiBella came over, embraced me, and kissed me on both cheeks. (Don't get me wrong, we weren't fags or nothing. It was just our way of showing respect.)

"Joey, I want you to know how much I enjoyed that meal," the acting Don said to me. "I know it was some kind of southern dish, because Little Dom tells me you're from the south. So where exactly in South Brooklyn you from?"

I kid you not. The guy may have been a boss, but he was still a lob at heart. Now, a lot of the boys had brought dessert with them from a variety of Italian bakeries. But since this was Little Dom's "Scoutmaster," I really wanted to do it up. So before anyone could get to cutting open the store-bought desserts, I had the waiters bring out my famous Rice and Ricotta Pudding.

Rice and Ricotta Pudding

FILLING

> *4 cups whole-milk ricotta cheese (2 15-ounce containers; Polly-O brand preferred)*
> *1 cup sugar*
> *1 tablespoon grated lemon peel*
> *1 ounce semisweet chocolate, melted*

$\mathcal{B}$eat ricotta and sugar (with electric beater) until creamy. Mix in lemon peel and chocolate. Set aside.

PUDDING

> 1⅛ cups rice
> 6 cups milk
> ¾ cup sugar
> 3 eggs
> ¾ teaspoon vanilla
> Butter for coating baking dish
> Flour for dusting
> 1 tablespoon ground cinnamon

$\mathcal{C}$ombine rice, milk, and sugar in large saucepan. Bring to boil, uncovered, over low heat. Simmer, uncovered, for 20 minutes from boiling point, stirring frequently. Remove from heat. Reserve ¼ cup of rice pudding liquid (skimmed from top) in small bowl. Cool along with pudding for 20 minutes. Beat eggs and reserved liquid until blended (do not overbeat). Trickle into rice mixture, stirring well. Add vanilla. Generously butter a high, 12-inch round baking dish and dust with flour. Spread about half the pudding on bottom of baking dish. Spread ricotta cream filling over pudding and cover with remaining pudding. Bake in preheated 325-degree oven for 1 hour 15 minutes. Serve hot or cold, sprinkled with cinnamon.

Menu

New York Strip Steak Florentine
with Sautéed Mushrooms
Asparagus Hollandaise

HALLANDALE, FLORIDA, 1976
TOMMY AGRO'S APARTMENT

PEOPLE PRESENT:

Joe Dogs   Tommy Agro
Skinny Bobby DeSimone
Louie Esposito   Buzzy Faldo

....

*T*t was T.A.'s coming-out party. He'd just done eight months—mostly in the hospital ward because of his asthma—and this was his first night back in Florida. He'd asked me, Skinny Bobby, Louie, and Buzzy over, and I'd told him his wish was my culinary command. Like any guy fresh from the joint, he wanted steak. (Tip for would-be *compares:* if any guy wants to join your crew and tells you he's just out of the joint, take him to dinner. If he orders anything but steak or lobster, he's lying and probably a Fed.)

New York Strip Steak Florentine with Sautéed Mushrooms

3½ tablespoons butter

2 teaspoons olive oil (extra-virgin or virgin preferred)

2 pounds mushrooms, cleaned and sliced

Salt and pepper to taste

2 tablespoons chopped fresh chives (or 1 tablespoon dried crushed chives)

3 tablespoons chopped fresh parsley

3 cloves garlic, sliced paper thin with single-edge razor blade or crushed and chopped fine

1 shallot, chopped fine

¼ cup cognac

Juice of ½ lemon

5 New York strip steaks, 8 ounces each

eat butter and olive oil in large frying pan over medium to high heat. When hot, add mushrooms and 1 teaspoon salt and ½ teaspoon pepper. Cook for 10 minutes, stirring or tossing occasionally. Add chives, parsley, garlic, and shallot, stirring them in to blend for 7 or 8 more minutes. Then add cognac and lemon juice. Allow to simmer for 5 more minutes, stirring occasionally. Taste and check for seasoning. Broil steaks to your preference (rare preferred) and pour sautéed mushrooms over steaks. Mushroom recipe is for 5 steaks. I like to serve this with a nice asparagus in hollandaise sauce. Just serve the sauce on the side if it's too rich.

Asparagus Hollandaise

4 egg yolks
¼ teaspoon dry mustard
¼ teaspoon salt
¼ teaspoon white pepper
Juice of ½ lemon
½ pound (2 sticks) butter, melted and clarified by pouring off milky residue
1 bunch asparagus spears (approximately 20 stalks), trimmed and steamed

lace egg yolks, mustard, salt, pepper, and lemon juice in blender and blend at high speed for 1 minute.

Then put on low speed and slowly add clarified butter until mixture thickens. *Very important:* Do not scorch butter, and pour only the clarified butter—not any milky residue—into blender. Pour over steamed asparagus stalks. *Serves 4.*

"Joey, these mushrooms are so good," Tommy said in the calmest voice I'd heard in years. The joint must have done him good.

"You gotta be careful with mushrooms, though, Tommy." Skinny Bobby always had to put in his two cents. "Some of them are poisonous."

"Yeah, I know," I said. "I lost my first wife that way."

Tommy was seriously taken aback. "Jeez, Joey, I didn't know that. You never said nuttin'."

By this time I was almost in tears. "Yeah, I lost my second wife, too. From a crushed skull."

"Marrone," T.A. said. "What happened? Car accident?"

"Nah . . . She wouldn't eat the poison mushrooms."

Menu

Manicotti Marinara with Mint

HALLANDALE, FLORIDA, 1976
TOMMY AGRO'S APARTMENT

PEOPLE PRESENT:
Joe Dogs
Tommy Agro
Skinny Bobby DeSimone
Louie Esposito
Buzzy Faldo

*T*here was a broad in Tommy's apartment this afternoon, and Tommy was always trying to show me off if he thought it would help get his worthless little ass in the sack. She said her name was Jennifer—Jenny, the crew started calling her—and I must admit, she was a looker. She'd shown up at the apartment peddling Stanley Products door-to-door. You know, shaving cream, toothpaste, razor blades, stuff like that. She had samples with her, and you'd order from her catalogue. Personally, I suspected she was a hooker with a great angle. No matter. It wasn't like any of us were averse to popping a hooker.

Anyway, right away T.A. starts in with his lord-of-the-manor routine. "Jenny, honey, I want you to meet my personal chef, Joey Dogs. You're gonna stay and have dinner with us, Jenny. What're you selling? *Marrone*, what a body you got there. You ain't selling that, are you? Ha ha. Just kidding. Joey, cook up something special for my little Princess Jenny here. Hurry up, Joey! Jenny's hungry!"

Like I need this, right? Tommy was making Skinny Bobby and Louie buy a lot of junk from Jenny when I left for the kitchen to whip up a little manicotti for her highness.

Manicotti Marinara with Mint

CREPES

1 cup flour
1 cup plus 2 tablespoons water
2 eggs

*B*eat flour, water, and eggs well to make batter. Pour, ⅛ cup at a time, into slightly heated and greased 9-inch frying pan (batter should make 8 to 10 thin crepes). Rotate frying pan to distribute batter evenly. Cook until bottom of crepe is just dry and crepe can be removed from frying pan with rubber spatula (top of crepe should remain moist). Lay crepes flat in clean work area until batter is used up.

"Yes, honey, put Bobby down for a case of shaving cream. Louie too." Tommy's largesse from the living room.

"But Tommy," Jenny protested, "there's twenty-four tubes to a case, at $4.95 a tube. That's a lot of money."

"Don't you worry, Jenny, honey, both these lobs shave two, sometimes three times a day. Right, boys?"

The crew muttered their assents as I snuck back into the kitchen, but not before I heard T.A. put me down for a case too.

Hey, it's only money, right? I began making the cheese filling for the manicotti.

CHEESE FILLING

> *1½ cups whole-milk ricotta cheese (Polly-O brand pre-*
> *ferred)*
> *¼ pound mozzarella cheese, diced*
> *½ cup freshly grated Parmesan cheese*
> *12 to 15 fresh mint leaves, well chopped*
> *Salt and pepper to taste*
> *Marinara Sauce (see page 16)*

Mix the three cheeses, chopped mint leaves, and salt and pepper in a bowl. Spoon evenly into center of crepes. Roll crepes and fold the ends underneath, leaving seam on bottom. Spoon a few tablespoons of marinara sauce into bottom of casserole dish and spread evenly. Place crepes on top of sauce, and spoon rest of marinara sauce on top of crepes. Cook in preheated 325-degree oven for 20 to 25 minutes. *Serves 4 to 5.*

After dinner Tommy totaled up Jenny's bill. We owed her $893.84, "without the sales tax." Jenny said she'd get back to us with that, seeing as she'd forgotten her calculator. Tommy threw her a grand and told her to forget about the change.

Later, after a couple of hands of pinochle, T.A. took Jenny to see Lou Rawls in the Tack Room of the Diplomat Hotel in Hallandale. When I stopped by to pick him up on the way to the track the next morning, Jenny was just leaving.

"See, Joey, she wasn't no hooker. She didn't ask for nothin' this morning. I don't pay for _____."

"You don't pay for it, Tom? What do you call free dinner, Lou Rawls, drinks all night at the Dip! Not to mention one thousand dollars worth of _____ing toothpaste?"

"*Minchia*, Joey, that ain't paying for it. That's business."

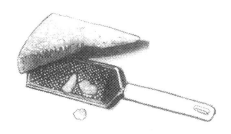

Menu

Giambotta
(Green Beans, Potato, and Tomato)

WEST PALM BEACH, FLORIDA, 1977
MY HOME

PEOPLE PRESENT:
Joe Dogs
Billy Ray (Colombo associate and hitman)

*B*illy Ray loved his wife so much he killed her. Billy was part of Little Dom's crew in New York. Stone cold. Dominick had sent him down to help me "persuade" a used-car dealer in Hollywood Beach that his health was in danger if he continued to beat up the daughter of a friend of ours. Billy Ray was a real good persuader.

Anyway, we'd just taken care of business in Hollywood (satisfactorily, I might add) and I invited Billy back to my house for dinner. My wife, Bunny, was visiting her mother for a week, and I decided to throw together a dish of giambotta. Billy followed me into the kitchen. That's when he told me how he'd whacked his wife. Hey, nothin' like a cozy chat while puttering around the kitchen, right? So Billy talked while I put together the ingredients for the giambotta.

Giambotta

4 to 5 cloves garlic, finely chopped
½ cup olive oil (extra-virgin or virgin preferred)
1 (35-ounce) can peeled tomatoes
Pinch of crushed dried oregano
2 medium to large boiling potatoes
Approximately 2 cups green beans (or sliced zucchini)
Salt and pepper to taste

A few years back, Billy began, he'd married his childhood sweetheart. Their honeymoon was interrupted when Billy had to go in for an eighteen-month stretch for assault. "When I came home," Billy continued, "I found out she was ____ing one of my so-called friends. From the first day I went into the can! I couldn't believe it. I wouldn't believe it. So I decided to test her. Told her I had to go to California on a piece of work, and that I'd be gone a week, maybe ten days. I promised to call her every night. The first night I call her from Los Angeles and tell her I love her. You know what she says to me, Joey? 'Ditto.' Ditto, Joey! Can you ____ing believe that? I knew he was there in bed with her."

I told him to save the rest of the story for dinner. I only hoped that I'd have an appetite after hearing it.

*S*lowly brown garlic in olive oil. Drain liquid from tomatoes and chop them coarsely. Add tomatoes to browned garlic and oil and cook for 20 to 30 minutes over moderate heat, stirring occasionally. Add oregano. While this is cooking, parboil potatoes and beans separately. Cook beans until tender (or *al dente* if preferred), drain, and add to tomato mixture. Cut potatoes into 1-inch cubes, add to tomato sauce, and cook for another 5 to 10 minutes. Salt and pepper to taste. Giambotta can be served as a salad or an entrée. *Serves 2.*

As we sat to eat, Billy continued his weird "love story." He said that after he hung up with his wife he picked up a hooker and banged her for $200. The next day he made arrangements with the hooker to stay in his hotel room and, for another $500, to play a role in what he told her was a practical joke. Billy gave the hooker his home telephone number and asked her to call his house—collect from Billy—at midnight eastern time. Then he hopped a flight back to New York under a *fugazy* name and picked up a hot .45 with a silencer.

The giambotta was delicious, and Billy was talking with his mouth full. "I got to my house at about 11:20 p.m., parked a block away, and opened the front door with my key. I heard a bunch of rumbling around in the bedroom. I walked in, flipped the light switch, and there they were, trying to get dressed. I shot him twice in the head and once in the heart.

"She was so scared she couldn't speak. Believe me, Joey, I didn't want to kill her. I loved her so much. If she would have _____ed around with some stranger, I'd probably still be with her. But my close friend! I let her have the other three bullets in the head. Then I turned off all the lights and poured myself a drink. At midnight the phone rang. The operator said, 'Collect call to anyone from Billy,' and I accepted.

"I disguised my voice like a broad's for a few minutes, hung up, turned on the lights, put the television on loud, and flew back to California that night.

"Joe, I had the perfect alibi. They checked it out with the airlines, the hotel, the phone company. Everyone that knows me knows that I did it. Even the law knows. But go ahead, prove it. They can't. Joe, if it happened to you, I know you'd do the same. I had to do it to save face."

I poured this maniac another glass of wine and just kept my mouth shut.

Menu

Pasta Fagioli Appetizer Soup
Veal Osso Buco

MIAMI BEACH, FLORIDA, 1977
JOHNNY IRISH'S APARTMENT

PEOPLE PRESENT:
Joe Dogs
Dominick "Little Dom" Cataldo
Johnny "Johnny Irish" Mattera (Colombo soldier)
Tony Black (Colombo soldier)
Marcia and Lu Anne (hookers)

It was a celebration. Johnny Irish, a hitter in the Colombo *famiglia*, had just gotten his button. He'd been made, indoctrinated, accepted as an official soldier, which is all that any of us ever wanted out of life. Little Dom was down from New York to congratulate him. He'd landed in Palm Beach, picked me up, and driven me to Johnny's apartment in Miami. Johnny's *compare*, Tony Black, was also there. There were a couple of South Beach hookers at Johnny's place. One of them was named Marcia, and I immediately fell in love. So after examining Marcia in the back bedroom, I decided to show off my culinary skills by whipping up an Italian feast fit for a newly made man.

Pasta Fagioli Appetizer Soup

3 tablespoons olive oil (extra-virgin or virgin preferred)
3 slices bacon, cut into ½-inch pieces
3 or 4 cloves garlic, crushed and chopped fine
1 (16-ounce) can small white beans (Great Northern)
1 (8-ounce) can tomato sauce plus 1½ cans water
Salt and black pepper to taste
1 basil leaf
½ pound elbow macaroni, cooked and drained
1 cup freshly grated Parmesan cheese

*H*eat olive oil in medium saucepan and slowly sauté bacon and garlic until slightly browned. Add beans and sauté for 10 minutes, stirring occasionally. Add rest of ingredients except Parmesan cheese and simmer for 20 minutes. Mix cooked pasta into sauce. Discard basil leaf and serve while hot and soupy. Sprinkle Parmesan cheese over top after serving. *Serves 6.*

Veal Osso Buco

1 cup flour

Salt and pepper to taste

8 cross-cut veal shanks, 1½ inches thick

2 tablespoons corn oil

1 large white onion, chopped

4 cloves garlic, sliced paper-thin with single-edge
*   razor blade*

1 cup dry white wine

1 (28-ounce) can peeled tomatoes (Progresso Pomodori
*   Pelati con Basilico preferred), drained and chopped*

3 tablespoons tomato paste

¾ cup canned brown gravy

1 teaspoon crushed dried oregano

2 bay leaves, chopped

¼ teaspoon dried thyme

1 teaspoon Worcestershire sauce

½ teaspoon Tabasco sauce

1 teaspoon Accent (optional)

*M*ix flour with salt and pepper and dredge veal shanks in flour, shaking off excess. Heat corn oil in large frying pan. Sauté veal on both sides, approximately 4 to 5 minutes for each side, seasoning it as you turn it. Add onion and garlic and cook for another 3 to 4 minutes. Add wine and cook over a high flame for 3 to 4 minutes to burn alcohol off. Add tomatoes, tomato paste, and brown gravy. Stir and allow to boil. Add remaining ingredients. Place entire concoction in dutch oven or casserole dish, cover, and bake in preheated 350-degree oven for 2 hours 20 minutes. Remove veal shanks from mixture and cook sauce over high heat for 2 to 3 minutes. Pour sauce over veal shanks and serve. *Serves 4.*

After dinner my heart broke when Marcia went into the back bedroom with the man of the hour, Johnny Irish. But twenty minutes later, they were back in the dining room finishing their coffee. "Johnny must be like Superman in bed," I said to Tony Black. "Faster than a speeding bullet." Tony just smiled.

Menu

Savory Stuffed Artichokes Sicilian-Style, Breaded Sautéed Steak and Greens, Zabaglione

WEST PALM BEACH, FLORIDA, 1974
MY HOUSE

PEOPLE PRESENT:
Joe Dogs   Bunny (Joe Dogs' wife)
Tommy Agro   Sandi (T.A.'s girlfriend)

....

*T*his one's an oldie but goodie, and worth telling you about because it kind of says it all about the Mafia. I'd only been in Florida a year or two when a friend of mine named Louie Esposito introduced me to Tommy Agro, who was to become my mentor, my rabbi, my *compare*. T.A. was a squat, florid little man, standing five-foot-three on the tip of his toes. On this tiny frame he balanced a set of incongruously large shoulders, with a belly to match. He had a headful of straight black hair, combed back neatly, that must have looked beautiful on the horse it came off of. And though he wore elevator shoes to bring him closer to the sky, he was, still, always the last one to know it was raining.

I'd known T.A. about a month, and there was just something about him that made me want to be just like him. So one night I asked him over for dinner. It was me, Bunny, T.A., and one of his Florida girls, named Sandi, a black broad with the biggest set of knockers in the universe. Tommy liked knockers almost as much as he liked exotic broads. I rarely saw him with a white woman. It was always blacks, Asians, and even an Indian once or twice.

Anyway, I really knocked myself out trying to impress him. And I think my cooking on this night was really what smoothed my way into the Gambino crime family. We started with a delicious artichoke appetizer.

Savory Stuffed Artichokes Sicilian-Style

⅓ cup plus 4 teaspoons olive oil (*extra-virgin or virgin preferred*)
1 cup finely chopped onion
1 cup chopped fresh parsley
1 cup thinly sliced celery
1 large clove garlic, chopped fine
2 ½ cups coarse fresh bread crumbs
½ cup freshly grated Parmesan cheese
⅛ teaspoon pepper
Salt to taste
½ teaspoon crushed dried oregano
2 tablespoons freshly grated Romano cheese
4 medium artichokes

*H*eat ⅓ cup of the oil in 10-inch frying pan. Add onion, parsley, celery, and garlic. Cook 5 to 7 minutes (until celery is almost tender). Remove from heat and stir in bread crumbs, Parmesan, pepper, salt, oregano, and Romano. Take each artichoke and cut off stem, leaving flat base. Wash in cold water and drain. Spread leaves, making sure there is space in center for stuffing. Divide stuffing into 4 portions. Spread leaves on one artichoke and spoon three-fourths of one portion of stuffing into space in center, leaving approximately one-fourth to spread between leaves. Repeat process with each artichoke until all the stuffing is used. Stand artichokes upright in large saucepan containing 1 to 1½ inches of water and 1 teaspoon salt. Drizzle 1 teaspoon olive oil over top of each artichoke. Cover and cook for approximately 45 minutes, until tender. To check for tenderness, gently pull one artichoke leaf away. If leaf is removed easily, it's done. *Serves 4.*

"*Marrone*, Joey, these are good," T.A. said as he wolfed down the appetizer. I felt like a kid who's just gotten a straight-A report card. "Now listen to me, Joey. If you know anyone who wants a loan, you know, they pay the juice every week, you let me know. But they have to be solid, you know what I mean? And you can earn off the money, too."

I asked T.A. how much interest—or "juice," as he called it—he charged.

"Joey, it's all according to how much they want and what we can get without having problems. *Capisci?* Now, enough business. What's for dinner?"

Breaded Sautéed Steak and Greens

4 eggs
¾ cup olive oil (extra-virgin or virgin preferred)
2 tablespoons chopped garlic
Salt and pepper to taste
4 (12-ounce) strip steaks, ½ inch thick (trim excess fat)
1 cup flour
2 cups plain dry bread crumbs
Arugula, radicchio, and escarole leaves (enough to
*   make bed for steaks), tossed in olive oil, vinegar*
*   (enough of both to coat greens), salt, and pepper*

Beat eggs in mixing bowl. Add ½ cup olive oil, garlic, and dash of salt and pepper, and beat well. Dredge steaks in flour, shaking off excess. Dip steaks in, first, egg wash and then in bread crumbs. Sauté each steak on both sides in 1 tablespoon of remaining olive oil to desired doneness. Remove steaks. Placed tossed greens on individual plates and serve steaks on top to wilt greens. *Serves 4.*

"Tommy, I think I might know someone who needs a loan," I said over dinner. "A guy asked me the other day if I knew a shylock. I told him no, not here in Florida. But I could tell him about you and you take it from there. I think he wants $5,000."

"All right, Joey, now listen. If he mentions it to you again, tell him you know someone, but don't tell him who it is. Tell him it's five points a week. That's $250 juice a week. But don't tell him you know somebody. Wait until he asks you again. Believe me, Joey, he will. They all do. Now here's my home phone number in New York. Call me if he wants a loan. But you can call me anyway, to say hello, if you want."

I put Tommy's phone number in my wallet, but then took it out again and rewrote the number in code. I wanted to impress him. I wanted to be just like him. I wanted to be in the Mafia next to Tommy Agro, and I was ga-ga over the fact that I was doing something for him. T.A. had just become my idol, I thought, as Bunny cleared the table and I brought out dessert.

Zabaglione

PER PERSON:

2 egg yolks
2 teaspoons sugar
¼ cup Marsala wine (or sherry)
Fresh fruit (strawberries or raspberries preferred)

*B*eat yolks and sugar until well blended. Stir in Marsala or sherry. Place mixture in large bowl and place over medium heat. Whisk constantly while cooking until texture is thick (being very, very careful not to curdle). Pour over fresh fruit.

After dinner Tommy and I retired to the living room while the girls did the dishes. T.A. thought it was time for a heart-to-heart.

"Joey, I want you to relax," he began. "I know you're trying to impress me, but don't knock yourself out. I'm impressed with you. I'm impressed with your wife. I like the way you handle yourself. Now here's what I want you to do. Find yourself some more customers. Expand yourself. Do things. And if you have any problems, call me. I'll help you. But, on the other hand, if you do good, don't forget me. Because I have my own *compare*, and I can't forget him.

"In this life," T.A. continued, "when you eat alone, you die alone. Remember what I'm telling you. You think you knew people before? Forget about them. You belong to an organization now that is the biggest. Joey, when you're with me, there is no one in this _____ing world that can _____ with you. Not even the Pope. But there is one thing that I noticed that is one of your biggest detriments. You bring your wife along with you all the time, wherever you go. You got to stop bringing her around so much, Joey. It just don't look good."

Menu

Orecchietti with Peas and Prosciutto

LAKE WORTH, FLORIDA, 1978
LITTLE DOM'S CRASH PAD

PEOPLE PRESENT:
Joe Dogs
Dominick "Little Dom" Cataldo

*W*ake up, Joey, I'm flying in tonight." It was Dominick Cataldo's voice on the other end of the phone. "Pick me up at Lauderdale at nine-fifteen. I'm on Delta. You got to do something for me. I can't come dressed, so have some clothes for me and for you. *Capisci?*"

Little Dom was telling me he couldn't carry a gun on the plane and he wanted me to get us a couple. "What size jacket do you want me to bring?" I asked.

"I wear a thirty-eight," Dom said. "And listen, you know those slacks you got for my girl? She has a twenty-two waist. Bring them, too."

Later that night I picked up Dominick, he handed me an address in the Keys, and we drove south. I was packing two snub-nosed .38s and a little .22. Dom took one .38 and the .22 and stuffed them into his waistband.

"Dom, what the hell is coming down?"

"It's nothing, Joey. I just have to talk to some guys. I just need the pieces in case they don't hear so good. It'll only be a couple of minutes. In fact, you don't even have to turn the car off."

I found the place. Small ranch house–cum–fishing shack nestled inside a shadowy cove of bougainvillea. "Go around the block and park," Little Dom barked.

As I backed the car up, Dominick put on a long blond wig. Then he covered his face with a black beard and mustache.

"You go ahead," he said. "Drop me off on the corner, and after I go in, pull up in front of the house with the lights off and the car running. Don't ask no _____ing questions."

I didn't. I dropped him off and he minced up to the front door like a fag. I watched him enter, and once he got inside I began to pull up the car. I heard about twelve shots. Dominick came walking out and hopped into the passenger seat.

"Let's go," he said. "Take me to that safe apartment my *famiglia* keeps in Lake Worth and make me something to eat. That prosciutto thing you made last time sounds good." Who was I to argue? Here's my recipe for "that prosciutto thing."

Orecchietti with Peas and Prosciutto

½ pound thick-cut prosciutto, diced
½ cup olive oil (extra-virgin or virgin preferred)
1 tablespoon chopped onion
1½ cups fresh or frozen peas
1 pound orecchietti
2 tablespoons butter
½ cup freshly grated Parmesan cheese

*B*rown diced prosciutto in olive oil in a frying pan until crisp. Remove prosciutto with slotted spoon and set aside. Add onion to oil and cook until translucent. Add peas and cooked prosciutto and allow to simmer over extremely low heat while preparing pasta. Boil orecchietti until *al dente*. Drain pasta and place in large bowl. Add butter and cheese, a little at a time, while tossing pasta. Add pea and prosciutto mixture. Toss and serve. Again, this is a rich sauce—perfect for killer appetites. Ha ha. *Serves 4.*

～

Over dinner Dom told me that a couple of Colombians had beaten him and his *compare*, the Colombo capo Allie LaMonte, out of $80,000 on a dope deal. "I needed the disguise in the event someone else was there," he said. "And it was a good thing, too. There was a broad and two young kids."

"Dominick! You didn't?"

"Naw, Joey, I don't hurt kids or women. But without the disguise, I wouldn't have had no choice. Christ, I was hungry. Joey, this meal is delicious."

He just whacked a couple of guys and Dom was starving! Sometimes I couldn't believe the people I was hanging around with. On the way home I drove over a bridge and dropped the pieces into the Miami River. Then I needed a drink. I stopped at the Diplomat Hotel, caught the last show in the Tack Room, met a good-looking chick, and spent the night in a suite. I always got a room at the Dip dirt cheap. They gave me convention rates.

Pot Roast à la Joe Dogs

WEST PALM BEACH, FLORIDA, 1969
MY APARTMENT

PEOPLE PRESENT:
Joe Dogs
Bunny
Mike "Midge" Belvedere (Colombo associate and bookmaker)
Ann (Midge's wife)

y very first *compare* was Mike "Midge" Belvedere, a bookmaker from Long Island, New York. Midge was also connected to the Colombo crime family. Midge and his wife, Ann, were my son's godparents. Midge was a very good-looking guy, a bronze Sicilian with thick, wavy black hair and dark, dark eyes. Almost black. When he stared at you, you felt like knives were going through your head.

Midge's wife Ann was beautiful. She looked like Elizabeth Taylor but had a better body. But once she opened her mouth, *marrone,* you'd think she learned to talk at truck driver's school.

Soon after Bunny and I had moved to Florida, Midge and Ann flew south for a visit. I was still getting established, we were living in an apartment, we hadn't even bought our house yet, and money was a little tight. Not real tight, just a little. Anyway, the four of us were going out to see a late show, Sergio Franchi was playing a hotel in North Miami. But first I wanted to cook the Belvederes a great dinner.

Pot Roast à la Joe Dogs

Salt and pepper to taste
1 (3-pound) chuck roast (with bone in it)
5 carrots
5 celery stalks
1 large onion
4 Idaho potatoes (or 8 new, or red, potatoes)

1 (10 ¾-ounce) can cream of mushroom soup
   (Campbell's preferred) plus 1¼ cans water
1½ tablespoons Dijon mustard
1 tablespoon Gravy Master

*S*alt and pepper roast on both sides. Place roast in good-size pan and cook in preheated 400-degree oven for 20 minutes to brown. While meat is cooking, clean and cut carrots into 2-inch pieces. Repeat process with celery stalks. Cut onion into 8 pieces. Peel and halve potatoes. Mix mushroom soup and water in large bowl. Add mustard and Gravy Master for color and flavor. Mix well. Remove roast from oven and place vegetables around meat in pan. Pour sauce mixture over meat and vegetables, cover with aluminum foil, and bake for 2 hours at 350 degrees. Should be served with Dewar's White Label scotch on rocks. *Serves 4.*

Later, as the four of us were walking out of the Sergio Franchi show, the television actress Joi Lansing pushed through the mob waiting for the valet to retrieve the cars. Now Joi Lansing was best known for her, shall we say, awesome headlights. And as she approached our group, Joi smiled at Midge and sort of gave him the eye. Ann sidled up to her real slowly and said, "If you don't take your _____in' eyes off my husband, I'll smack you in the face with your own big _____, you _____in' whore."

Ann was beautiful. And she set the tone that first night for a wonderful time.

Chicken Cacciatore Northern-Style

HOLLYWOOD, FLORIDA, 1972
THE OLD PELICAN RESTAURANT

PEOPLE PRESENT:
Joe Dogs
Louie Esposito

$\mathcal{P}$erfect timing.

Louie Esposito was on the lam from another big robbery attempt. Louie was a great B&E man, and he'd gotten a tip about a house in New Jersey that was home to some $2 million in cash, stashed in some fake books in the library. Louie and a partner had dressed up as priests, faked a flat tire, and chloroformed the maid who let them into the house.

"We saw the ____ing money, Joey," he told me. "Stacked up in these empty books. A ____ load. But we musta tripped a wire. Within two minutes there were sirens and squad cars all over the place."

Empty-handed, Louie and the other guy ran into some woods behind the house and split up, and Louie spent the night in the rafters of an empty construction site. The cops caught his partner. Louie told me he was on the lam because he didn't know if the guy had given him up.

Coincidentally, not two nights before, me and my crew had busted up a joint, the Old Pelican Restaurant, on orders from Tommy Agro. The two brothers who owned the place were late with their vig. We hadn't torched the building, but it was closed. We'd really done a job—with sledgehammers and axes—on the bar and the dining room. But the kitchen was still intact. And there was an office with a cot.

Tommy Varaggo, one of the owners, had flown to New York for a sitdown with T.A. His brother Jimmy knew better than to come near the place. So I took Louie—who hadn't been present at the bashing two nights before—to the restaurant, tossed him the key, and told him to make himself at home. Then I cooked him dinner.

⚜

Chicken Cacciatore Northern-Style

2 to 3 tablespoons olive oil (extra-virgin or virgin preferred)
1 (2½-pound) chicken, cut into pieces
1 large onion, chopped into ¼-inch pieces
3 cloves garlic, crushed and chopped fine
2 shallots, chopped fine
½ cup dry white wine
1½ teaspoons red wine vinegar
Salt and pepper to taste
2 basil leaves (dried or fresh)

*H*eat olive oil in large frying pan. Sauté chicken over medium heat, turning occasionally, for approximately 20 minutes. While chicken browns, add onion, garlic, and shallots to pan. After 20 minutes or so, add wine, vinegar, salt, pepper, and basil to mixture. Cover tightly, and allow to simmer for another 30 minutes. Serve with pasta, rice, or vegetable. *Serves 4.*

Over dinner, something stuck in my craw (and not the chicken, which was delicious). Louie said he was on the lam from the Jersey robbery. Yet less than a year earlier his cut from the big Aqueduct Racetrack heist had come to close to a million bucks. When I asked him what happened to all that dough, a queer look kind of crossed his face.

"Are you kidding, Joey?" he asked. "My share was only $800,000. I went through that in a couple of months. Gee, though, I just wish I coulda paid off my house. Anyway, I have to find some work until I make another score. You got a job for me?"

Nobody in our organization could ever hold on to a buck. We all threw money around. Broads and more broads. Lawyers for pinches, bondsmen for bail. The lawyers got the most, though. We called them whores. They got that name from jumping from one client to another. I had a good lawyer. I got sentenced to a month one time. He got me out in thirty days.

Menu

Spinach and Eggplant Lasagna with Sun-Dried Tomato Sauce
Peach Cobbler

HOLLYWOOD, FLORIDA, 1980
NENA'S APARTMENT

PEOPLE PRESENT:
Joe Dogs   Tommy Agro
Popo Tortora (Genovese soldier and dope dealer)
Frank Dean (Genovese associate and Tortora's muscle)

*I*t was our version of going to the mattresses. Popo Tortora was a big doper with the Genovese family in south Florida, and he was at war with us. The problem was Popo's, though. He'd sold me some bad blow—six keys of coke—and I'd refused to pay. The crap wasn't fit to stuff up your ____, much less your nose, and I'd told Popo so. But he was making innuendoes like I'd switched his dope on him. Naturally, shots were fired. But nobody'd been hit. Yet.

The situation got so bad, however, that Tommy Agro had flown down from New York with some muscle after I got word that Popo was going to make a run at me at one of my hangouts, a restaurant owned by a friend of mine.

Anyway, six of us—all Gambinos—sat up all night at this restaurant, armed to the ____ing teeth, waiting for an attack that never came. Finally, one of Tommy's sluggers went hunting on his own and capped one of Popo's crew after a bar fight. That was enough for the big boys up in New York. This they didn't need. The Feds were coming down on us hard enough as it was, and they didn't want us fighting among ourselves and attracting atten-tion. So T.A.'s *compare*, the Gambino family *consigliere* Joe N. Gallo (not to be confused with Crazy Joey Gallo of the Colombos), ordered a sitdown.

We scheduled the meet at my girlfriend Nena's apartment in Hollywood. By this time my wife, Bunny, had tossed me out of the house for cheatin' like a jackrabbit. I was living with Nena, a real babydoll and a flight attendant for American Airlines with a body to die for. Luckily, she was on a West Coast turnaround when the meet went down.

Popo brought one of his top sluggers, a nasty piece of business named Frank Dean. T.A. and I ushered them in and frisked them. We'd laid our guns out on the living room couch, and expected them to do the same. Tommy had just been diagnosed with a heart condition, and didn't want any meat. So I went instead with a delicious, and meatless, lasagna. See how I looked after my *compare?* See what a nice guy I was? *Minchia,* if I had known how Tommy was gonna eventually look after me, I woulda shoved a twenty-ounce porterhouse down his throat. But I digress. Here's the recipe for the tomato sauce.

Spinach and Eggplant Lasagna with Sun-Dried Tomato Sauce

Tomato Sauce

> 8 cups chopped fresh plum tomatoes
> ½ cup sun-dried tomatoes (soaked in 1 cup water)
> 1 red pepper, seeded and quartered
> 1 onion, peeled and chopped
> 1 clove garlic, crushed and chopped fine
> 2 cups vegetable broth (or water)
> ½ teaspoon salt (or to taste)
> ½ teaspoon black pepper (or to taste)
> ½ cup fresh basil leaves, chopped

*C*ombine plum tomatoes, sun-dried tomatoes (and their liquid), red pepper, onion, garlic, and broth in saucepan. Allow to simmer, uncovered, for 45 minutes. Add salt and pepper to taste. As sauce is simmering—say, every 15 minutes or so—add basil leaves until all are used. *Makes 6 cups sauce.*

The sitdown wasn't as harrowing as I thought it would be. Granted, Frank Dean had a face and an attitude that could stop a train. But Popo was all smiles and backslaps. Popo was a scrawny old man, in his mid-sixties, and aside from dope he had a nice business going in forged airline tickets. He had someone inside at the airlines, and he could get you any ticket you wanted, on any carrier, at half price. As I was running back and forth between the kitchen and the living room he must have offered me free tickets ten times. I also heard him telling Tommy that he was sure our "little squabble" could be solved amicably, and after it was, he was going to call over the most gorgeous hookers either of us had ever seen. Now, because of his doping, Popo always had broads galore. And I liked a good hooker as much as the next guy. But this wasn't a good sign. If there was one thing I'd learned by now about T.A., it was that his little head always did all his thinking for his big head. And I didn't need his little head getting in the way of any negotiations. This was as good a time as any to put together the lasagna.

LASAGNA

> *5 medium eggplants, cut into ⅜-inch rounds*
> *2 to 3 teaspoons salt*
> *2 teaspoons fresh thyme (or ½ to 1 teaspoon dried)*
> *1 bunch spinach, stemmed, washed, and lightly steamed*
> *4 cups low-fat ricotta cheese (Polly-O brand preferred)*
> *2 cups chopped fresh basil leaves*
> *1 egg*
> *1 teaspoon black pepper*
> *Tomato Sauce (recipe above)*
> *12 dry lasagna noodles (or pre-boiled, if preferred)*
> *1 (8-ounce) package mozzarella cheese, thinly sliced*
>   *(optional)*

Sprinkle eggplant with 2 to 3 teaspoons salt (depending on taste and heart condition). Set aside in colander to drain for 30 minutes. Rinse and pat eggplant dry. Combine eggplant and thyme in nonstick frying pan over medium to low heat. Cook, a few at a time, on both sides until barely tender. Place in bowl and set aside. Also set aside lightly steamed spinach. Combine ricotta, basil leaves, egg, and salt and pepper to taste and set aside. Spread 2 cups of tomato sauce along bottom of 9- by 9-inch baking dish. Place 4 uncooked lasagna noodles over sauce. (*Note:* Pre-boil if pasta is preferred well done, as noodles will be *al dente* if cooked dry in recipe.) Top with a third each of spinach, ricotta mixture, and eggplant and 1 cup sauce. Repeat procedure twice, ending with a layer of sauce. Add top layer of thinly sliced mozzarella (optional). Cover with foil and bake in preheated 350-degree oven for 45 minutes. Remove foil and bake an additional 15 to 20 minutes.

During dinner Tommy started bragging to Popo about how healthy he'd been eating. "How do I look, Popo?" he'd ask. "Don't I look thinner?" Popo, who wasn't much interested, nodded his assent. Then, after we were done, Tommy said—in all seriousness—"Well, I may be thinner, but I feel like I'm eating like a ____ing rabbit. Joey, you got any bacon and eggs and toast back there? I need some meat." About this time I was wishing he'd die of a heart attack right there.

As it was, we straightened out the dope dispute over dessert, a tasty peach cobbler I'd thrown together especially for the occasion. Popo agreed to call a truce if we could help him lay off the bum dope. T.A. knew a couple of knockaround Lucchese guys who sold to college kids—college kids never know good dope—and agreed to contact them. The hookers showed in time for coffee and the cobbler. Sweets for the sweet, right? A week later all was back to normal.

Peach Cobbler

6 to 8 fresh peaches, peeled
Confectioners' sugar and cinnamon to taste
1 cup flour
½ teaspoon baking powder
⅛ teaspoon salt
½ pound (2 sticks) butter, softened
1 cup granulated sugar
1 egg, beaten
½ teaspoon vanilla

*M*ix peaches with desired amount of confectioners' sugar and cinnamon in bottom of 9- by 13-inch baking pan. Mix together flour, baking powder, and salt. Cream together softened butter and granulated sugar and add to flour mixture. Fold in egg and vanilla. Spread cobbler mixture over fruit and bake in preheated 375-degree oven for 35 to 40 minutes. Dust with additional confectioners' sugar and serve with ice cream while cobbler is still warm.

P.S.: Two years later the Feds issued a narcotics-trafficking indictment on Popo Tortora. They came to arrest him at his hotel in Miami. He was sunning himself at the pool. When he saw the G approaching, his heart seized up and he died right there in his lounge chair. We should all be so lucky.

Menu

Fish en Papillote
in Béchamel Sauce

North Miami Beach, Florida, 1980
Jiggs Forlano's Apartment

People Present:
Joe Dogs
Jiggs Forlano

*T*heir big mistake was trying to scam a scammer. To make a long story short, I was still living with Nena when Bunny called to say our house had been robbed. It turned out it was just some neighborhood kids, but I took the insurance company for all I could get, including a claim that my wife's $10,000 diamond ring had been stolen. Of course, I had hidden the ring real good before I claimed it was missing.

At any rate, the insurance company made good, and I picked up a replacement ring from a Miami jeweler. But a few months later, when I went to hock the piece, my pal Jiggs—the "retired" Colombo capo and a jewelry expert—informed me that it was costume. I hit the roof. Jiggs agreed to accompany me to the jewelry store, because he knew the people who ran it.

Jiggs and I walked into the jeweler's separately, with Jiggs walking to a corner, pretending to be window shopping. He was carrying a small fishing gaff under his coat. He told me that if anyone gave me a problem he'd be more than happy to rip their eyes out. I walked to the counter and signaled to the guy who had originally sold me the stone. I'd called before, so they knew I was coming.

"Here's your piece of glass, you crooked _____," I said.

"Don't talk to me that way," this guy says. "Who do you think you are? I'm giving you $6,000 for that ring, and no more."

With that, I reached over, grabbed this moron by the tie, and backhanded him. Then I pulled his head down onto the jewelry case, cracking the thick glass. He started bleeding from the nose and mouth. Just then, Jiggs appeared at my side. "Hi, Joe," he said, smiling amiably and flashing the gaff. "You got a problem here, or what?"

"No, Jiggs, I don't think so. My friend here has a nosebleed, and I'm trying to tell him what's good for it."

The clerk recognized Jiggs, nodded hello, ran back to his office, and came back with a $10,000 check. He'd left the name blank.

I said, "Listen, get one of your flunkies to cash this check right away. I want cash, *capisci?*"

He went back to his office, returned with the cash, and ordered a salesgirl to bring me a solid-gold bracelet. "Keep it, with our compliments." Later, I mailed Tommy Agro $2,000 and the bracelet. When I earned, T.A. earned.

On the drive back to Jiggs' place in North Miami I slipped the old capo a grand for his trouble. Then I made him dinner, his favorite, Fish en Papillote in Béchamel Sauce.

Fish en Papillote in Béchamel Sauce

BÉCHAMEL SAUCE

> *5 tablespoons butter*
> *5 tablespoons flour*
> *4 cups hot milk*
> *Salt and pepper to taste*
> *Pinch of grated nutmeg*

*M*elt butter in saucepan. When hot, add flour and stir for approximately 2 minutes. (Important: Do not scorch!) Pour in 1½ cups of milk and stir with whisk over low heat. As mixture comes to boil, slowly add rest of milk and the salt, pepper, and nutmeg. Cook for approximately 15 minutes over low heat, stirring occasionally.

～

FISH

> *2 pompano fillets (can also use red snapper)*
> *Salt and pepper to taste*
> *Papillote bag (purchase in specialty supermarket)*
> *1 teaspoon chopped shallot*
> *1 tablespoon chopped celery*
> *3 tablespoons Béchamel Sauce (recipe above)*

*S*eason your fish with salt and pepper and place fillets in bag. Add all other ingredients and tie bag tightly with accompanying tie. Bake in preheated 350-degree oven for 20 minutes. The bag will rise but will not tear. When serving, pierce bag with knife and pour onto plate (or over rice) with all the juices. *Serves 2.*

Menu

Baked Chicken à la Joe Dogs

LAKE GEORGE, NEW YORK, 1980
THE HOLIDAY INN

PEOPLE PRESENT:
Joe Dogs
Brooke (Joe's girlfriend)
Dominick "Little Dom" Cataldo
Lorraine (Little Dom's girlfriend)

$\mathcal{T}$'d been a member of Tommy Agro's Gambino crew for over ten years now. In spite of T.A.'s warnings, I was double-banging him behind his back. It just didn't seem right that I could only earn from one *famiglia*. It was undemocratic. So when Little Dom called from New York and wanted to know if I could score him some pot, I didn't think twice about doing business with the Colombos. The Gambinos always looked down on the Colombos anyway, like they were junior members of the mob. And it's a fact that they did a lot of the Gambinos' dirty work. Most Colombos were crazy. So I felt like I was working with distant relatives, though I know Tommy wouldn't have seen it that way.

Anyway, I scored 580 pounds of Colombian Gold for $130 a pound and sent it north to Little Dom with Billy Ray on the autotrain, and three weeks later Dom called to say he'd offered the entire consignment to one guy at $285 a pound. We made $45,000 apiece, which called for a celebration. Dom suggested I grab a broad and meet him in Lake George, beautiful country in the summertime.

I flew up the next day with a cute little honey I'd just met named Brooke and met Dom in his luxury suite. He was there with his girlfriend Lorraine. I hadn't seen Dom in a while, and it was a happy reunion. The night was so beautiful, the air so sweet, that I didn't feel like fixing any heavy Italian food. We settled on baked chicken, the perfect summertime dish.

Baked Chicken à la Joe Dogs

4 chicken breasts (remove skin but leave bones in)
1 tablespoon pepper
2 or 3 (to taste) cloves garlic, crushed and chopped
2 teaspoons crushed dried oregano
4 new (red) potatoes cut into ¼-inch rounds (leave skin
    on)
2 small onions, quartered
1 tablespoon garlic salt
1 tablespoon Accent (optional)
2 cups chicken stock
1 (15-ounce) can sweet peas

*P*lace chicken breasts, facing bone down, in 14- by 10-inch baking pan or dish. Sprinkle pepper, chopped garlic cloves, and oregano over meaty tops. Arrange potatoes and onions in pan around chicken. Sprinkle garlic salt and Accent (optional) over top of everything and pour 1 cup of chicken stock over chicken breasts. Cover pan or dish and cook in preheated 350-degree oven for 45 minutes. After 45 minutes, remove cover and pour the other cup of chicken stock, as well as can of sweet peas, including juice, over concoction. Bake, uncovered, for another 20 to 25 minutes. Serve with rice and Dewar's White Label scotch. *Serves 4.*

After dinner Brooke raised her eyebrows when Dom pulled out a peanut butter jar filled with cocaine. He began drawing lines on the glass table and handed me a straw. He knew I didn't do that stuff, but I guess he was testing me. I declined. So he snorted some and Lorraine snorted some, but Brooke was hesitant. So to put her at ease I snorted a line, but Brooke still refused.

We went to the lounge for a few drinks, but after taking that snort I began to feel nauseated. I excused myself and went to the men's room to upchuck. When I returned the girls were gone. Dom said they'd been in the ladies' room for quite a while. "I bet Lorraine turns Brooke on," he added. I didn't care one way or the other. It was her nose and her business. But Little Dom was right, because when the girls came back Brooke was talking a mile a minute.

During one of the girls' many subsequent trips to the ladies' room, Dom leaned across the table and told me a secret. "My friend Johnny Irish has a big problem," he said. "He led the FBI from Florida to where the boss was on Long Island." Dom was referring to Carmine "the Snake" Persico. "Now the Snake is really pissed off."

I was stunned. Dom was telling me that Johnny Irish was probably not long for this world. I told Dom I didn't want to know any more, and he didn't bring it up for the rest of the evening.

But that night, driving back to our hotel room with Brooke, Johnny Irish was all I could think about. In our business, they'd turn on you and have you capped in a minute. Did this mean that Little Dom or Tommy Agro, my two best friends in the world, could someday turn on me? Brooke talked like a jackrabbit all the way back to our room. That's not all she did like a jackrabbit that night. And I was surprised. Brooke was a natural blonde.

Mussels in Light Sauce

QUEENS, NEW YORK, 1980
LITTLE DOM CATALDO'S APARTMENT

PEOPLE PRESENT:
Joe Dogs
Dominick "Little Dom" Cataldo
Carol (Little Dom's girlfriend)

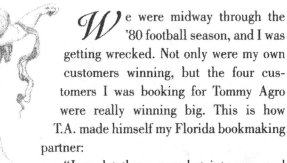

*W*e were midway through the '80 football season, and I was getting wrecked. Not only were my own customers winning, but the four customers I was booking for Tommy Agro were really winning big. This is how T.A. made himself my Florida bookmaking partner:

"Joey, let these guys bet into you, and you keep the tabs. We'll split the winnings. But if they win, I'm out. I'm not your partner no more."

So it went, "belonging" to Tommy Agro.

So I got shafted. What's new? October. November. December. I took a major bath. I was tapped. And not only was I losing in football, I was also getting killed at the track. So it was a godsend when Little Dom called from New York and told me he'd gotten rid of some coke I'd shipped him during the past summer. My end came to 150 large, and I told Dom I'd be on the next flight to New York to collect.

That night, Little Dom and I were divvying up the cash in his girlfriend's apartment in Queens when he told me to make a shopping list for dinner. I was in the mood for mussels, and Dom sent the broad out to pick up the food. By the way, those ten pounds of mussels are no mistake—these are guys with hearty appetites. And that goes for some of the broads, too.

Mussels in Light Sauce

10 pounds fresh mussels, scrubbed clean
4 cloves garlic, smashed
¼ pound (1 stick) butter
4 dried chili peppers, crushed
¼ cup chopped fresh parsley
Juice of 1 lemon
¼ teaspoon pepper
1 cup dry white wine
2 tablespoons cooking sherry
1 cup peeled tomatoes, drained and chopped
4 tablespoons chopped fresh parsley
½ teaspoon dried crushed oregano
8 chopped fresh bay leaves or crumbled dried bay leaves

*P*lace mussels in a big pot, add 2 garlic cloves, ½ stick butter, chilies, parsley, lemon juice, pepper, and water ½ inch above mussels. Cover and bring to boil. Remove mussels when shells open, which should take about 15 minutes. Pour juice from mussels into a frying pan and set mussels aside. Melt remaining ½ stick butter in pan containing mussel juice. In pan, sauté remaining garlic for approximately 1½ to 2½ minutes, or until limp. Add wine and sherry and cook for another 3 minutes over high heat. Add chopped tomatoes, parsley, oregano, and bay leaves and cook for 12 minutes over medium to high heat, stirring several times. Place mussels, still in shell, on baking tray. Pour tomato mixture over mussels and bake in preheated 400-degree oven for 4 additional minutes. Serve with garlic bread and pasta. *Serves 3 or 4.*

After our delicious feast, Dom walked me out to his car and told me I had to do him a favor. "Let's take a ride," he said.

"Sure, Dom. What is it?"

"I have to go up the Taconic Parkway and dig a hole," he told me. "I got this mother____ in the car and I need a hand getting him into the hole. I'll do the digging. I just need a hand getting him out of the trunk. I just can't leave him in the streets, Joey. This guy was a made man with the Lucchese family."

He had to be kidding. I began backing away from his car. "Dom, you're not serious, right? You don't really have a ____ing body in the trunk, do you?"

"Hey, Joe, what the ____'s wrong with you?" he said. "Why would I tell you a story like that?"

With that, he popped the trunk. There was a body inside, all right, all twisted up. The hole in this poor sap's forehead had already formed a bloody scab. I felt sick. I wished I hadn't cooked mussels. I had to get out of there.

"Joey, this guy's been in my trunk for three days now, and he's starting to stink. I need a hand. What do you say?"

"Dominick, I'm going to tell you like T.A. would say it. I wasn't made with a finger. What do you want to do, make another two-story job? ____ you! Get someone else to help you. I don't want to know where your burial grounds are."

"Yeah, Joey, I guess I can't blame you," he finally said after a long, icy moment. "But that's not what I had in mind, honest. Not to worry, I'll get someone else to help."

"Yeah," I said, "and make sure it's somebody you don't like." And with that, we hopped a cab to the nearest bar.

Menu

Just Desserts

WEST PALM BEACH, FLORIDA, MARCH 1981

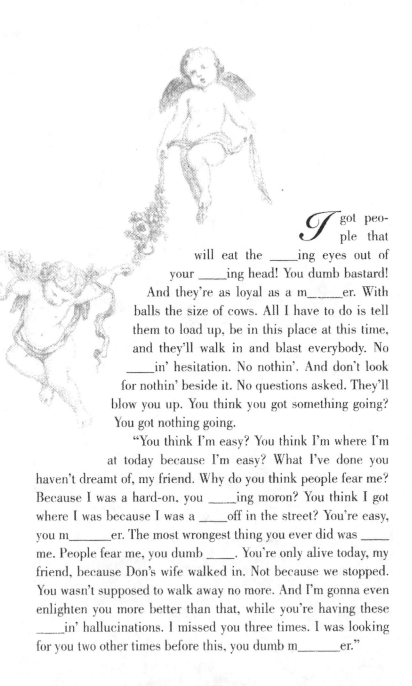

$\mathcal{I}$ got people that will eat the ____ing eyes out of your ____ing head! You dumb bastard! And they're as loyal as a m____er. With balls the size of cows. All I have to do is tell them to load up, be in this place at this time, and they'll walk in and blast everybody. No ____in' hesitation. No nothin'. And don't look for nothin' beside it. No questions asked. They'll blow you up. You think you got something going? You got nothing going.

"You think I'm easy? You think I'm where I'm at today because I'm easy? What I've done you haven't dreamt of, my friend. Why do you think people fear me? Because I was a hard-on, you ____ing moron? You think I got where I was because I was a ____off in the street? You're easy, you m____er. The most wrongest thing you ever did was ____ me. People fear me, you dumb ____. You're only alive today, my friend, because Don's wife walked in. Not because we stopped. You wasn't supposed to walk away no more. And I'm gonna even enlighten you more better than that, while you're having these ____in' hallucinations. I missed you three times. I was looking for you two other times before this, you dumb m____er."

That was the apoplectic Tommy Agro, calling me from New York. You might say we'd had a falling-out. I lay in my bed, holding the telephone receiver at arm's length, listening to T.A. screaming at the top of his lungs. My head ached. My broken ribs burned like kindling. And my nose, splayed across my face, was split down the middle. To T.A.'s dismay, I was still alive. Barely.

Six weeks earlier, Tommy A. and two of his sluggers had flown south with the intention of beating me to death. They'd used a baseball bat and a lead pipe, and the last thing I remember before losing consciousness was Tommy digging his dainty little alligator loafer into my ribs. And all because I was a lousy three months late on my vig! I'd only survived through fate. Just as T.A. was about to chop off my right hand with a meat cleaver—Mafia symbolism—Don Ritz's wife had walked into the kitchen of Don Ritz's Pizzeria on Singer Island, where the beating had taken place, and let out a bloodcurdling scream. She'd spooked the sluggers, and they'd fled.

I'd awakened three days later in St. Mary's Hospital. The priest giving me last rites called it a miracle. My mother and daughters were there in the hospital room. As well as my wife and my girlfriend. And FBI agents Larry Doss and Gunnar Askland.

Now, six weeks later, Tommy was letting me know he hadn't cooled down. I sipped my scotch, smiled, and watched the tape recorder attached to the telephone unspool. The tape recorder was courtesy of the Florida FBI. But the revenge was going to be all mine. The Feds had dubbed our gig "Operation Home Run," because of the way they'd used my head for batting practice. They should have called it "Operation Tunnel Vision," because I was going underground with one thing in mind. Getting even.

Menu

Steak au Poivre

LAKE WORTH, FLORIDA, 1981
MY NEW APARTMENT

PEOPLE PRESENT:
Joe Dogs
Tony Amoroso (FBI supervising agent)
Larry Doss (FBI agent)
Gunnar Askland (FBI agent)
Rossi (FBI agent)

*J*oey, we're bringing in a new agent to go undercover with you," said Case Agent Larry Doss. "That's what Tony wants. And he wants you to pick the agent you feel most comfortable with. Tony's bringing over someone tonight for you to meet. So what are you cooking for dinner?"

I was sitting in my new apartment in the backass end of Lake Worth, far from the madding crowd and far from the Mafia, which two months earlier had tried to kill me. With me were FBI agents Larry Doss and Gunnar Askland, my case agent and his assistant. The Eye was paying for this apartment and everything in it, including me. I was now working for the Feds, with one thing on my mind. Revenge. I wanted to see Tommy Agro buried.

Doss and Askland's supervisor, Special Agent Tony Amoroso, was on his way over. I had convinced Tony that if he could just get me straight, monetarily, with T.A., I could worm my way back into the mob's good graces. I'd wear a wire. I'd tap telephone calls. I'd do anything to nail T.A.'s ass. Amoroso agreed, on the condition that I work with some backup. Tonight, he was bringing a potential undercover over for dinner. I was making Steak au Poivre, for five. The key is how you make the veal stock, which you have to do a day ahead of time.

Steak au Poivre

VEAL STOCK

> ¼ cup olive oil (extra-virgin or virgin preferred)
> 2 or 3 veal bones (butcher will cut for you)
> 1 gallon water (enough to cover bones in pot)
> 4 celery tops
> 6 to 10 tomato ends
> 2 onions
> 2 carrots
> 2 tablespoons tomato paste

*H*eat olive oil in 8-quart stockpot and brown bones. When browned, add just enough water to cover bones and throw in vegetables. Bring to a boil and allow to simmer, uncovered, for anywhere from 12 to 24 hours (24 preferred). As water evaporates, replace. Two hours from finish, add tomato paste. Now allow water to evaporate. When you get to about half the liquid you started with, it's done. Strain and freeze in 1-cup portions for later use.

Supervising Agent Tony Amoroso showed up with the undercover agent as I was setting the table. He had to be joking! The guy Amoroso brought in, an agent named Rossi, was Italian all right. But he looked to be about sixteen years old. *Marrone.*

STEAK

3 tablespoons olive oil (extra-virgin or virgin preferred)
½ cup crushed peppercorns
5 (8- to 10-ounce) filets mignons
1 cup Veal Stock (recipe above)
2 ounces cognac (Rémy Martin preferred)
3 tablespoons heavy cream
Salt and black pepper to taste

W hile olive oil heats in large frying pan, press peppercorns into both sides of steaks. Cook steaks in olive oil to your desired doneness (rare preferred). Remove steaks and place in 150-degree oven to keep warm. Add stock and cognac to olive oil and meat drippings in pan. Step back and ignite. After flame burns out pour heavy cream into mixture and cook over medium heat for roughly 5 minutes until mixture is reduced by half or less, stirring repeatedly. Season with salt and pepper while stirring. Spoon some sauce onto each plate. Place steaks on top of sauce and spoon remaining sauce over top of steaks.

Agent Rossi was professional, and he was anxious, and as we wolfed down our steaks I gave him the lay of the land. "These aren't just kids or bank robbers we're dealing with here," I explained. "They're hardened criminals and killers. If you think for one minute that if they find out you're an FBI agent you're safe, forget it. They'll chop you up and then grind up the parts so no one will ever find you. They'll flush you down the toilet and your friends here will be burying an empty casket."

Then I played for Agent Rossi Tommy Agro's infamous "eat the ___ing eyes out of your ___ing head" tape.

"What's wrong, Agent Rossi? Don't you like my steak? You look a little pale. You want to lie down?"

Agent Rossi didn't pass the screen test. He'd never be able to hack it. He knew it. We knew it. No hard feelings.

Menu

Shrimp Scampi Gambino-Style

HALLANDALE, FLORIDA, 1982
POOLSIDE AT THE DIPLOMAT HOTEL

PEOPLE PRESENT:
Joe Dogs
Tommy Agro
Checko Brown (Colombo soldier)
Anthony "Fat Andy" Ruggiano (Gambino capo)
Skinny Bobby DeSimone
Paulie Principe and Frank Russo (Gambino associates and sluggers)

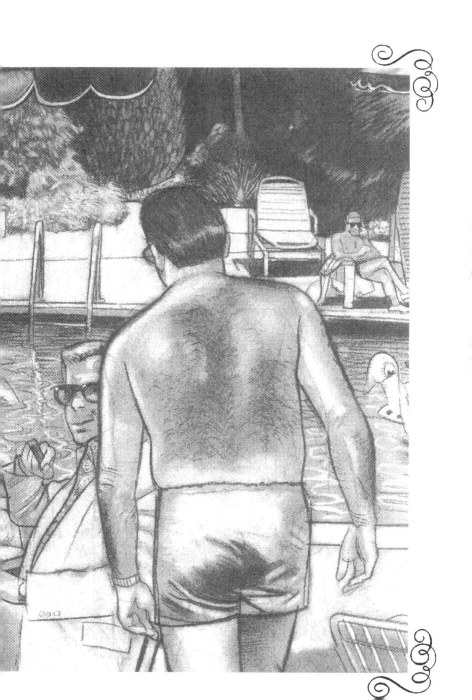

*T*ommy Agro called at midnight.

  I was now in the habit of pressing the "record" button whenever I picked up the phone. I always made sure there was a fresh tape in the machine. The only person I didn't tape, I wouldn't tape, was Little Dom. It was part of the deal.

"I'm here, Joey, at the Dip. Come and see me tomorrow."

"I'm hurt, T.A.," I whimpered. "I'm hurt bad. Please don't hurt me anymore. I didn't do anything wrong. Can't it be over? Can't we start fresh?"

My begging was not a facade. I was really afraid. I hadn't seen Tommy since the beating—five weeks ago—and I dreaded facing him so soon. My head was still a mess. The scars from the stitches were still raw.

"Joey, I'm not gonna do nothin' to you," he said. "I'm down here for somethin' else. Believe me, it's all over. I'll never do that again."

On the drive down I–95 that morning I watched the Feds tailing me through my rearview mirror. I'd wanted to wear a wire, but they'd forbidden it. Said it was too dangerous so soon. The valet at the Dip barely recognized me, my head was so swollen. The Olympic-size pool was packed with tourists. Tommy's cabana, complete with kitchen, was at the south end, near the wading pool. My stomach sank when the first guys I saw were Paulie Principe and Frank Russo, the two sluggers who'd helped Tommy beat me to a pulp. Then I spotted Checko Brown, the Colombo soldier, talking to Fat Andy Ruggiano, the Gambino capo. Bobby DeSimone, fresh from a stint in the joint, was sitting next to T.A. I stopped in my tracks and started to tremble. I was frozen to the pavement. Tommy came hurrying over.

"Joey, don't worry, relax. Didn't I tell you we wasn't gonna do that no more? Come over here, say hello to the boys. Cook us some food, Joey. We're sick of this hotel _____."

We made small talk for a while, then Tommy asked me to make the boys lunch. But first, he added, why didn't I put on a swim suit. "I got an extra," he said. "It's hot out here, Joey. It'll be hotter over the stove. Checko, get Joey a suit."

It was an odd request. Checko was fully dressed. So was DeSimone. Nevertheless, Checko and I walked to the cabana and Checko found the suit. I got undressed in front of him. The only place a wire could have been was up my rear. Checko didn't check there. In the kitchen I started deveining the shrimp, watching Checko walk the fifteen paces or so back to the boys. When he reached them, the crew looked at me, then at Checko.

"*È pulito,*" Checko said. *He's clean.* What the hell? Did this moron think I didn't understand Italian? Forgive and forget, right, Tommy? Enjoy the scampi, boys. And don't choke on 'em.

Shrimp Scampi Gambino-Style

2 pounds shrimp (preferably under 15 to a pound)
¾ pound (3 sticks) butter, softened
3 shallots, chopped fine
4 cloves garlic, crushed and chopped fine
Juice of ½ lemon
2 tablespoons chopped fresh parsley
½ cup plain dry bread crumbs
1 egg yolk
1 teaspoon Accent (optional)
2 teaspoons Red Devil hot sauce
Salt and pepper to taste

*C*lean, devein, and butterfly shrimp. Place them in large, flat pan. Mix butter, shallots, garlic, lemon juice, parsley, bread crumbs, egg yolk, Accent, hot sauce, and salt and pepper to taste in bowl. Spoon over raw shrimp. Place under broiler for 3 to 5 minutes, checking occasionally so that they do not overcook. Spoon excess melted sauce over shrimp and serve. *Serves 5. Add more shrimp for more people.*

Over lunch, with me still in my bathing suit, everyone talked a little more freely and came a little closer to me—except Principe and Russo, who stayed in the pool. I'd made the right move not wearing the wire. Business could now commence.

Lobster Newburg

SINGER ISLAND, FLORIDA, 1982
MY NEW APARTMENT

PEOPLE PRESENT:
Joe Dogs
John Bonino (FBI agent, Joe's undercover partner)
Larry Doss
Gunnar Askland

I knew Agent John Bonino was going to make a good undercover partner when, over a delicious meal of veal and pasta marinara, I pulled my "chop you up and flush you down the toilet" routine on him and his only reply was to ask me what ingredients I put in my marinara sauce.

Bonino was out of the Eye's Chicago office, and the Feds in Washington were grubstaking us to an illegal after-hours club we'd use to sting the Florida mob. The bottle club was equipped with all kinds of surveillance cameras, and since I was now back in T.A.'s good graces, the Feds figured we'd pick up all kinds of good information. I passed John off as my money man—everyone knew I was broke since the beating—an old friend who wanted to get out of the drug-smuggling business and into a "legit" operation. The bottle club was the perfect cover.

I was cooking for Bonino, Agent Larry Doss, and Agent Gunnar Askland in my new apartment in a high-rise on Singer Island. The Feds had sprung for apartments for me and John in the same building. Over cocktails, I mentioned to the agents that I'd been coming out of my barbershop on the Island that afternoon when I'd seen a car drive through the parking lot. A wiseguy named Skeets was driving, Johnny Irish was in the front passenger's seat, and Tony Black was in the back. Nothing particularly odd. But there's nothing particularly odd about this special dish, either. Sweet lobster with a rich béchamel sauce. *Perfetto* for those quiet evenings at home with the Feds.

Lobster Newburg

3 tablespoons clarified butter, melted and clarified by
    pouring off milky sediment
½ teaspoon paprika
¼ cup cooking sherry
1 quart Béchamel Sauce (see page 89)
2 basil leaves
4 to 6 drops yellow food coloring
Pinch of salt
¼ teaspoon white pepper
1 teaspoon chicken base or 2–3 chicken bouillon cubes
    dissolved in ¼ cup water
1½ pounds lobster meat (Maine preferred)

Put 2½ tablespoons clarified butter in medium saucepan and heat until bubbly (don't burn) over low flame. Add paprika and whisk vigorously. Add sherry, ignite, and cook alcohol off. When alcohol has evaporated, add béchamel sauce and stir until blended. Add basil leaves and simmer for 20 minutes (do not boil). Add food coloring, salt and pepper, and chicken base and simmer for additional 10 minutes, stirring occasionally. Remove basil leaves. Coat separate frying pan with remaining butter and sauté lobster meat, stirring constantly. When hot, remove lobster and add to sauce. Simmer for additional 5 minutes and serve with yellow rice or rice pilaf. *Serves 4.*

Midway through dinner the phone rang in my bedroom.

"Hello?" Out of habit I pushed the "record" button on my nightstand.

"I didn't think you were home. You usually get the phone on the first ring." It was Little Dom. Once I heard his voice I stopped the tape from recording.

Dom told me to expect an invitation to his son's upcoming wedding, and we were just making small talk when out of nowhere he asked cryptically, "My friend Johnny, down south there, you know who I mean?"

He meant Johnny Irish. "What about him?"

"He's gone, Joey. Gone."

"Are you kidding me, Dominick?"

"Hey, Joey! I don't joke about something like that. My *compare*, Donny Shacks, he told me about six o'clock tonight that he was gone."

"Dom, he's got to be mistaken," I said. "I saw him with Tony Black and Skeets, driving around Singer Island late this afternoon. Around four o'clock."

"Hey, Joe, what the _____ is wrong with you?" Dom said. "I don't give a _____ if you saw him at five-thirty. He's gone. *Capisci?*"

I hung up the phone, went back to the dining room, and announced to the Feds that Johnny Irish had been whacked. We all skipped dessert. And nobody was ever charged with Irish's murder.

Menu

Caponata

WEST PALM BEACH, FLORIDA, 1982
DON LUIGI'S RESTAURANT

PEOPLE PRESENT:
Joe Dogs
Tommy Agro
Fat Andy Ruggiano
Skinny Bobby DeSimone
Frank Russo
Paulie Principe

ommy Agro showed up at Don Luigi's with the capo Fat Andy Ruggiano and the rest of his crew in tow. Bobby DeSimone. Paulie Principe and Frank Russo— the boys who, along with Tommy a few months earlier, had tried to shuffle me off this mortal coil. Don Luigi's was owned by Don Ritz, a member of my crew, and I felt pretty safe there. I was wearing a wire. At first T.A. didn't like having Ritz around because he thought he was Jewish. The mob is the most prejudiced group around, after all. But when I explained to Tommy that "Ritz" was a shortened Italian name, he cooled down.

Don Ritz got everyone seated in a private room in the rear of the restaurant and I headed off to the kitchen to prepare my famous caponata, one of Tommy's favorites. While I was cooking, Don Ritz, a stutterer, joined me. He looked nervous.

"Christ, Joe, I can't believe these guys," he stammered. "They come down here, beat you, leave you for dead, and then they want you to cook for them? I wou . . . wou . . . wou . . . wouldn't do it."

I laughed to myself. Don was a real nice guy. He had a heart of gold and he ran a fine restaurant. All he wanted to do in life was make good pizzas.

"Yeah, Don, that's just how they are," I joked. "I hope they like the caponata, because they sure didn't like the fettuccine I made. They almost killed me over it."

"I don't know how you can joke around like that," Don said. "Don't you hate them?"

"Nah. Why should I hate them? By the way, Don, you got any arsenic around here? I'm going to kill the whole group."

"Joe, quit _____ing around," he said. "I just got this joint. I got a lot of money stuck in here. If you want to whack them, please do it somewhere else."

Don Ritz's stuttering became even more pronounced when Bobby DeSimone walked into the kitchen. "Joey, Joey," DeSimone said in that fag voice of his. "I was just telling Tommy that you make the best caponata I ever tasted. Can I watch?"

"I'm glad you like it, Bobby, but listen, this ain't my joint. So you can't hang around back here. You'll get in the chef's way."

As DeSimone walked back out, I said loud enough for him to hear, "Don, hand me that stuff I wanted to mix into the sauce."

You could almost see the light bulb going off over Skinny Bobby's head. He half turned, looked at me suspiciously, and continued out.

"Wh . . . wh . . . why did you say that?" Don stammered. "Now he's gonna tell them there's poison in the sauce."

"_____ 'em, I said. "Let 'em sweat a little bit."

Caponata

¾ *cup olive oil (extra-virgin or virgin preferred)*
2 *large onions, chopped into ¼-inch cubes*
4 *cloves garlic, smashed and chopped fine*
½ *pound prosciutto, sliced and cut into ½-inch pieces*
2 *slices bacon*
2 *cans jumbo black olives, pitted and sliced (each can*
    5¾ *oz. drained)*
½ *cup heavy cream*
1½ *pounds perciatelli pasta*
1 *cup freshly grated Parmesan cheese*
3 *egg yolks, beaten*

*H*eat olive oil in large frying pan. Add onions and garlic and sauté until translucent. Add prosciutto and bacon and cook until bacon is crisp. Remove bacon and discard. Add olives and cook until very soft, stirring often. With a slotted spoon, remove all ingredients to a bowl and pour cream into olive oil. Whisk with wire whip until texture develops. Return all ingredients to pan. Sauce is finished. Keep hot. Meanwhile, pasta should be boiling. Cook it *al dente*. Drain, but do not rinse. Put pasta back in pot. Add Parmesan cheese, toss, and stir. Add egg yolks slowly, tossing pasta as you do so until pasta is thoroughly covered. Place on large platter, spoon sauce over pasta, and serve. *Serves 6.*

I spooned the sauce over the perciatelli and told Don to serve it to the crew while I washed up. He brought it out and three or four minutes later walked back into the kitchen smiling. "They want you to eat with them," Don said without a stutter. "They're waiting for you before they start."

I walked out of the kitchen with a grin. "C'mon, fellas, dig in."

"After you," Fat Andy insisted. "Here, Joey, let me put some on a plate for you. I mean, after all, you did all the cooking and we want to show our appreciation. Honey? Honey, bring Joe Dogs a nice scotch. Dewar's, isn't it, Joe?"

Andy filled my dish and told me to dig in while he and the other guys filled their plates. I took a couple of healthy bites and licked my chops. Everyone stared.

"Aren't you guys going to eat?" I asked as I filled my mouth again. They started eating, and the compliments began rolling in.

Bracciole

NORTH MIAMI BEACH, FLORIDA, 1982
FAT ANDY RUGGIANO'S HOUSE

PEOPLE PRESENT:
Joe Dogs   John Bonino
Fat Andy Ruggiano   Sal Reale (Gambino soldier)
Ronnie "Stone" Pearlman
Junior "Fingers" Abbandando
and Gerry Alicino (Gambino associates)
Skinny Bobby DeSimone

*F*BI agent John Bonino—aka drug smuggler John Marino—and I were invited to the Gambino capo Fat Andy's house to pick up a $25,000 shylock loan. We'd told him we needed it to start our illegal gambling joint—disguised as a "bottle club"—in Riviera Beach. It would turn out to be the largest illegal loan ever taken by an undercover Fed from the Mafia, and John would get lots of awards for it. It would also be introduced as evidence, later, during Fat Andy's racketeering trial.

Fat Andy's crew met us in his driveway. There was Sal Reale, a made member in Fat Andy's gang. And Ronnie "Stone" Pearlman, who could only be an associate because he was a Jew. (The Mafia not being an equal-opportunity employer.) Junior "Fingers" Abbandando, who got a discount at the manicurist because he only had nine fingers, was there. Bobby DeSimone and Gerry Alicino were standing on the porch.

The crew had met John once, and they were at ease, so we talked about the club, the different prices for building materials, where to get blackjack and roulette tables, that kind of thing. John and I were both wearing Nagra body recorders.

After an hour, Fat Andy asked me to join him in the kitchen to whip up some grub. Sal Reale followed me in.

"Joe, just how well do you know this guy John?" Reale began. There was a menace to his voice. "We're giving him the loan only because of you. You understand that, don't you? Your friend T.A. said that you're tops with him. So that's why we're doing it."

"Well, if Tommy said all these nice things about me, what the _____ are we talking about here?" I bluffed, turning to Fat Andy. "Did you bring me in here to read me the riot act or to cook dinner? I feel insulted, Andy. Look, forget the loan. I'll get it for John somewhere else. See you at the club."

I turned for the door and felt a hand on my shoulder. I almost crapped in my pants. I was sweating so much I was afraid I'd short-circuit the Nagra. It was Fat Andy's paw.

"Joe, don't feel insulted." He was being conciliatory. "Sal didn't mean no harm. He just asked you one little question, that's all. Come on now, shake hands, and make us something nice to eat."

Sal and I shook hands, and laughed. "*Marrone,* what a hothead," he said as he tried to hand me the money.

"Sal, do me a favor," I said. "Give it to John. It'll make him feel respected if you were to hand it to him and make the arrangements about the vig."

"Okay, Joe. After dinner."

Bracciole

¼ pound (1 stick) butter, melted
2 tablespoons olive oil (extra-virgin or virgin preferred)
8 (4-inch) pieces eye or bottom round steak, pounded
    thin with mallet
Salt and pepper to taste
4 cloves garlic, smashed and chopped fine
1 cup plain dry bread crumbs
½ cup chopped fresh parsley
4 hard-boiled eggs, chopped
Tomato Sauce (recipe on page 128)

Rub mixture of butter and oil into one side of each piece of meat. Rub salt and pepper into same side. Spread layer of chopped garlic over same side. Cover garlic with layer of bread crumbs. Cover bread crumbs with layer of parsley. Cover parsley with layer of chopped eggs. Roll and tie with sewing string (or secure with toothpicks). Fry over medium heat approximately 3 to 4 minutes until brown all over. Remove from frying pan and simmer in tomato sauce for 2 hours. *Serves 4.*

Over coffee Sal made a big show of handing John the money. Then they settled on the vig—a very reasonable two points a week. "Why choke the guy?" Fat Andy asked magnanimously. Little did he know who would eventually be choking on that loan.

Menu

Stuffed Shells with Tomato Sauce

KEW GARDENS, QUEENS, NEW YORK, 1983
TOMMY AGRO'S HOUSE

PEOPLE PRESENT:
Joe Dogs
Tommy Agro
Tommy Agro's geisha girl

$\mathcal{T}$ he phone was ringing as I walked into my hotel suite in Queens at eleven a.m., the morning after Sammy Cataldo's wedding—Sammy was Little Dom's kid. Tommy Agro was on the line, summoning me to his home.

Tommy had a beautiful mansion in Kew Gardens, Queens, with two marble fireplaces, including one in a master bedroom measuring one thousand square feet, and a spacious and spotless kitchen. Tommy's wife Marian was now his ex-wife, and T.A. kept the house stocked with a bevy of exotic broads. I was shown into the living room by a comely little geisha.

"Here's $1,200 for four weeks, Tip," I said, handing him his juice. "I know the last week isn't due yet, but since I'm up here you might as well take it."

"Yeah, thanks, Joey," he answered gruffly. "Let's throw together some lunch, and then we gotta talk." Something was definitely bothering him. Maybe my stuffed shells would soothe the savage beast. This is a three-part recipe—the meatballs for the tomato sauce, the sauce itself, and the cheese filling for the shells. It takes time but is definitely worth the wait and effort.

Stuffed Shells with Tomato Sauce

MEATBALLS

1 pound ground beef
1 small onion, diced
3 cloves garlic, smashed and chopped fine
1 egg
¼ cup ketchup
½ cup plain dry bread crumbs
Salt and pepper to taste

*M*ix all ingredients together and form meatballs. Set aside.

TOMATO SAUCE

3 tablespoons corn oil
Meatballs (recipe above)
1 pound sausage, cut into 3-inch pieces
2 (28-ounce) cans peeled tomatoes (Progresso Pomodori
    Pelati con Basilico preferred), crushed
1 cup chicken stock
2 (6-ounce) cans tomato paste
2 cups water (or chicken stock)
Salt and pepper to taste

*H*eat oil in pot over low flame. Sauté meatballs and sausage, turning occasionally, until browned (turn gently, so as not to break meatballs). Add tomatoes and cook over low heat for 45 minutes, stirring occasionally. Once tomatoes have cooked, add chicken stock, tomato paste, and 2 cups water (or additional chicken stock). Stir gently to blend. Add salt and pepper to taste, and cook for 4 hours on low flame.

SHELLS AND FILLING

> *1 pound jumbo shells*
> *3 cups whole-milk ricotta cheese (Polly-O brand preferred)*
> *½ pound mozzarella cheese, diced*
> *3 eggs*
> *2 tablespoons chopped fresh parsley*
> *Salt and pepper to taste*
> *⅓ cup freshly grated Parmesan cheese*

*B*oil shells, drain, and run cold water over them. Mix ricotta, mozzarella, eggs, parsley, and salt and pepper in bowl. Put filling into each shell. Place thin layer of tomato sauce along bottom of baking pan. Place shells on top of layer of sauce and pour remaining sauce over shells. Sprinkle grated Parmesan over everything. Cover with foil and bake in preheated 350-degree oven for 15 to 20 minutes. *Serves 4 to 6.*

. . . .

As it turned out, this was one fabulous culinary creation that I never did get to eat . . . at least not that day at Tommy's house. For while the sauce was simmering, T.A. started fulminating.

"Listen, Joey, who's this guy you brought up here with you?"

"He's a good friend," I answered. "Name's John Marino. From Chicago. And I know him longer than I know you. What's on your mind, Tip?"

"What's on my mind is you're sure he's all right? I mean, you don't have any illusions that you think you can bring a cop around here to try and get in with us, do you, Joey?" I had to hand it to T.A. His instincts were good, and sometimes he wasn't as dumb as he looked.

"Look, Tom, in all due respect, I didn't come here to be insulted, all right?" I said. "I told you who he was. If you'd like to check him out, be my guest. It would give me great pleasure to get an apology from you. John is my partner in the *babonia.* I earn off the guy." *Babonia* was our word for drugs.

"So this guy's your dope partner, huh?" Tommy growled. "Well, let me tell you something, Joey, and I'm only gonna tell you once. The boss, Big Paulie, he's put out the word. No more drugs. He just had three made guys from Neil's side of the *famiglia* whacked for dealing in that _____. They were all with that c_____er Gotti's crew."

T.A. was rolling now, as only T.A. could when he worked himself up into one of his apoplectic fits. His face was purple. The words were bursting out of his mouth at the top of his lungs. It was a good time to look for a place to hide. I saw none.

"So, Pippie, don't make me have to tell you no more. Understand? Find some other way to earn. And if that guy John continues to do it, you're going to have to answer for him. So tell him. *Finito! Capisci?* Don't let me find out different.

"And don't bring him around me. I don't want to meet him. Fat Andy likes him? That's fine. Put him with Andy. But you belong here, Joey, *capisci?* You aren't going anywhere. But tell that guy John if he ____s with drugs, he's going bye-bye and you're the one who's gonna send him off.

"Now get out of here. You make me lose my appetite. Go back to Florida and earn. Send me some money, you hump."

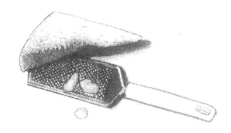

Menu

Bouillabaisse

SINGER ISLAND, FLORIDA, 1983
MY APARTMENT

PEOPLE PRESENT:
Joe Dogs
John Bonino
Robbie (Colombo associate)

*T*hree days after Christmas Robbie called. Robbie hung around Freddie Campo—one of the biggest bookmakers in south Florida. As part of the FBI sting operation, I was splitting a bookmaking halfsheet with him. John Bonino, the undercover, had all the agents calling in and making football bets, for evidence. Anyway, I'd told John that a few years earlier, Robbie had called me one day around three in the morning and said that a local lob named Stanley Gerstenfeld had been whacked. Stanley was a tough-guy wannabe and degenerate gambler. The State's Attorney had called me in for questioning about Stanley's murder because I'd brained Stanley in a local saloon a few weeks before he was capped, but I had an airtight alibi. The murder was still listed as "unsolved" on the Florida books.

At any rate, Robbie was the writer and collector on our bookmaking sheet, and it was time for our weekly payoff meeting. John told me to ask Robbie over for dinner and try to get him to open up about Stanley's murder. Robbie was an egomaniac, and I figured it wouldn't be too hard to pull his chain. He was in a good mood when he arrived, and after he paid me my vig I opened a bottle of scotch. John and Robbie made small talk while I threw dinner together. A nice fish stew for someone who someday may sleep with the fishes.

Bouillabaisse

¼ cup olive oil (extra-virgin or virgin preferred)
10 to 15 live blue crabs (quickly pre-boiled and cleaned)
3 cloves garlic, smashed and chopped
½ pound squid
1 pound shrimp (25 to 30)
12 to 15 clams
12 to 15 mussels
1 pound any nonoily fish (optional)
2 (28-ounce) cans Italian tomatoes (Progresso
    Pomodori Pelati con Basilico preferred)
1 pound linguine
Salt and pepper to taste

*H*eat olive oil in large pot. Place crabs and garlic in pot and toss or stir for 10 minutes. Place lid over pot and simmer for another 10 minutes. Add all other ingredients—except pasta—and cook over medium flame for 30 minutes, stirring often. Boil pasta, drain, and pour bouillabaisse over pasta. *Serves 4.*

As we were eating and talking, I brought up the subject of the late Stanley Gerstenfeld. "You know, Robbie," I said, "Stanley had a hunch that something was wrong, because before he died he kept trying to reach me. In fact, he did reach me, and wanted to talk to me, but we never got together. I think he knew what was coming."

"He didn't know a _____ing thing," Robbie spat out, like a true tough guy. "When I put the bag over his head, *then* he knew he was going. I put three or four in his head, and one in his heart so he wouldn't bleed all over the car."

"Oh, does that stop the bleeding?" I asked, playing dumb.

"Yeah, Joey. You're putting me on. You know it does."

This entire conversation took place right in front of John, who did the right thing by sitting there nice and quiet, just listening and letting that little Nagra tape recorder roll under his shirt. We got the whole thing on tape. But the authorities never went after Robbie—maybe it was just a good story. Who knows?

After Robbie left I mentioned to John that, deep down, Robbie was nothing less than a maniac. "Did you hear him say he wishes he was Italian?"

"More Italians like him we don't need," John answered. "We need some nice quiet ones, like your pal Tommy A."

Menu

Veal Oscar

HALLANDALE, FLORIDA, 1983
TOMMY AGRO'S HOTEL SUITE

PEOPLE PRESENT:
Joe Dogs
Tommy Agro
two Chinese hookers

ommy called at the end of January. He was down south in his suite at the Dip, and he wanted me pronto. He had two Chinese hookers with him and he needed me to cook dinner. What began as an ordinary evening—I didn't wear a wire that night; too dangerous—ended in an epiphany. But first we ate. Tommy had the hotel's kitchen send up everything I needed for my four-star Veal Oscar with hollandaise sauce.

Veal Oscar

4 veal cutlets
2 tablespoons olive oil (extra-virgin or virgin preferred)
2 (8-ounce) cans crabmeat
1 bunch fresh spinach, stemmed, washed, and steamed
Hollandaise Sauce (recipe on page 47)

auté veal in olive oil in frying pan approximately 2 minutes each side. Remove crabmeat from can and layer over veal. Layer spinach over crabmeat. Bake for 5 minutes in preheated 350-degree oven. Remove, place in serving dish, spoon hollandaise sauce over top, and serve.

After dinner, Tommy handed the hookers a roll of cash and sent them down to the hotel's shopping arcade. He had business to discuss. I'll never forget the conversation that followed.

"Listen, you _____in' suitcase, there's something I want to tell you," he barked in that soft-spoken manner of his. "But you have to promise me that it doesn't go any further than this room. Because if it does, it'll make me look bad, and I'll have a bad taste in my mouth."

"Who would I tell?" I asked, throwing up my hands and cursing myself for not wearing the Nagra.

T.A.'s face turned serious. "Joey, I didn't want to hurt you the way I did," he said. "It wasn't my fault. My *compare*, Joe Gallo, made me do it. It wasn't me, or the money you owed me. He just used that as an excuse to get to you. I swear, Joey. It wasn't me."

I was stunned. "But why would Gallo want to hurt me? After all the money he made with us on the dope? On the racetrack scam? And what about the beating I gave that guy up in Naples because of his little _____ing bitch? The guy whose sister he was dating, the one who didn't want him around?"

"Stop, Joey! Stop right there! I told you once before never to talk like that about my *compare*. Besides, that's the reason. That guy you _____ed up, the zip with the sister. You _____ed him up too much. You wasn't supposed to hurt him that bad. That girl, Sophia, she left my *compare* over that. It's been eating at him ever since, and he blames you."

I was flabbergasted. I'd been maimed, I'd almost been killed, I'd gone to work for the Feds, all because of Joe Gallo's little bitch on the side! It couldn't be. Tommy had to be lying.

After a long pause, T.A. continued. "What can I say, Joey? Except that my *compare* wanted you *morto*. It's a good thing Don

Ritz's wife walked in or right now you'd either be dead, or with no right hand."

"You should have shot me, Tommy," I cried. It wasn't an act. "You should have killed me. I didn't deserve to be left like that. I've been nothing but loyal to you for over ten years. And look at me. I'm _____ed up! I look like a freak! I can't even eat without cocking my head. I don't even feel the liquor I'm drinking. I got a lump on my forehead the size of an orange. All this because Joe Gallo blames me for losing his little _____? A man would have killed me, Tommy. A man wouldn't have left me like this."

For once Tommy Agro was speechless. He just stood there shrugging his shoulders. I wheeled and stalked out of the room. I didn't feel like a hooker that night. Not even a Chinese one.

Menu

Maine Lobster Fra Diavolo
Lemon Granita

HALLANDALE, FLORIDA, 1983
TOMMY AGRO'S HOTEL CABANA

PEOPLE PRESENT:
Joe Dogs
Tommy Agro
Skinny Bobby DeSimone

*J*oey, I'm down here at the Dip. Bobby's with me. Meet me by the pool. I got to see you about my *compare*'s thing." T.A. sounded calm.

It had been two months since Tommy'd informed me that I'd nearly been beaten to death on orders from his *compare*, the Gambino family *consigliere* Joe N. Gallo. Ever since, I'd been burning with revenge to nail both of those bastards. Luckily, fortune struck. My Colombo *famiglia* pal Little Dom Cataldo had gone away on an armed-robbery beef, but before he went in he asked if I had any connections to get him an easy prison stretch at one of the federal country clubs. Dom had made the request because he knew my girlfriend Nena's father was a big muckety-muck in Washington, D.C. But, instead, I'd taken Dom's request to my new associates in the Eye, and they'd arranged for Little Dom to do his time at Allenwood Federal Penitentiary, the crème de la crème of soft time.

The Feds were hoping that Dom would spread the word throughout the mob that Joe Dogs could fix prison sentences, thereby enabling them to build a racketeering case against anyone who bit. Their plan worked like a charm. No sooner was Dom plunked down in Allenwood than the Colombos had me make similar arrangements for Carmine "the Snake" Persico, who wanted to serve his time close to New York. For $20,000, my "connection" would arrange it. And then Tommy Agro called me about Joe Gallo's kid, who was doing hard time in Attica, a snake pit in upstate New York. Gallo wanted his son transferred to a softer pen, and, per the FBI's instructions, I played along with the sting. This offshoot of Operation Home Run came to be known as the Favors case. There was only one problem. The Colombo organization had failed at first to come up with the scratch for the Snake, and the Feds, pissed off that no money had changed hands, had had Dom transferred to Kentucky, where he was doing hard time. I felt bad about that.

T.A. and Skinny Bobby were drinking coffee by the cabana when I arrived at the Diplomat Hotel. T.A. thought I was pulling prison strings through Nena's connection in Washington. His boss, Gallo, had arranged to get his kid transferred out of Attica for $20,000.

"Bobby's got the money in the hotel safe," Agro began. "Tell your friend in Washington we got the bread, but it stays right here until my *compare*'s kid is moved. Now, make us some lunch."

Maine Lobster Fra Diavolo

¼ cup olive oil

3 Maine lobsters 1¼–1½ pounds each, split in half and
    claws cracked

4 cloves garlic, crushed and sliced paper-thin with
    razor blade

1 (28-ounce) can Italian tomatoes (Progresso
    Pomodori Pelati con Basilico preferred), crushed

3 to 4 fresh basil leaves

Half (28-ounce) can fish stock (or water)

1 pound linguine

*H*eat olive oil in extra-large frying pan. Place split lobsters, cracked claws, and their juice in pan. Sauté for 5 minutes over medium heat, adding garlic as you turn lobsters. Add tomatoes, basil leaves, and fish stock (or water), cover, and simmer for approximately 12 minutes. Season to taste. Boil pasta (*al dente* is best), drain, and spoon lobster and sauce over individual servings. Goes best with a nice red chianti or burgundy. *Serves 3.*

〰

T.A. ate lobster like he did everything else. Like a pig. The guy needed a half-dozen bibs. During dinner the Nagra was pressing against my balls and killing me. I'd taken to wearing the tape recorder in my crotch—as opposed to my chest or back, because no true wiseguy would ever grab your ____. But after this conversation, I was glad I had it on.

"I feel so bad about Dominick," I told Tommy. "He's terrified of them big bad black guys in his cell block. And another thing, my connection in Washington is leery since he didn't get the money yet for the Snake. We got to make sure we do the right thing on Gallo's kid. *Capisci?*"

"Don't you worry, Joey, didn't I just tell you we got the money right here? You want to see it? You asking me to prove it to you?" I felt an Agro rampage coming on. "And another thing, my friend, if I was you, I wouldn't be worrying so much about the health of your great good friend Dominick Cataldo. Maybe he ain't as friendly as you think. Do you think I should tell him, Bobby?"

"Yeah, Tommy, I think you should tell him," DeSimone squeaked.

"What? What?" I asked. "Tell me what?"

"Tell you that your good friend Little Dom put a contract out on you," T.A. yelled. He let the words hang in the air for a moment. "Dom was taking credit for having the jailhouse juice. Then, when he got moved, it made him look bad with his *famiglia*. He wanted you dead. The guy Dom got to whack you came to my people for the okay, so we put a squash on it at a sit-down. So how do you feel about your good friend Little Dom Cataldo now?"

I was pretty shaken. But, truthfully, I also felt real good that the Nagra was rolling in my pants. It took me a minute to catch my breath. So Dom wanted me capped, huh? Well, ____ Little Dominick Cataldo. ____ him and the horse he rode in on. It was true. The Mafia has no friends, only interests. In that case I was going to enjoy my dessert.

Lemon Granita

½ cup sugar
2 cups water
6 to 7 lemons (enough for 1 cup of juice)

Make a syrup by mixing sugar and water in pot, bringing mixture to boil over medium flame, and boiling for 5 minutes. Turn off flame and allow syrup to reach room temperature. Mix with lemon juice and freeze in cups or pony glasses. (*Note:* the freezing process will take about an hour more than making ice because of the sugar content.) *Serves 3.*

Menu

Crabmeat Appetizers
Steaks Cognac

CAPE CORAL, FLORIDA, 1983
AN FBI SAFE HOUSE

PEOPLE PRESENT:
Joe Dogs
Larry Doss
Dick Gentlecore (FBI agent)
Roma Theus (Federal Prosecutor)

*B*y August of 1983 it was all over. Operation Home Run had closed down. Word had leaked to the Mafia from several sources—including one from the FBI's Washington headquarters—that someone in Florida was cooperating with the Eye. It didn't take a brain surgeon to figure out who that "someone" was. A third contract was put out on me. It was an "open" contract—anyone could collect. I don't know how much it was for.

Right before we closed down I'd flown to New York for one last sitdown with Tommy Agro. We'd met at a bar near the airport. The agents hadn't wanted me to go, but I insisted. Turned out to be a circus. The joint was crawling with mobsters and undercover Feds, who were very hard to pick out with their wingtips and white socks. Even Tommy had to laugh, after he'd had Fat Andy frisk me for a wire. I wasn't wearing the Nagra that night. No matter. T.A. knew. They all knew. I think they'd planned to cap me right there. But there were just too many cops in the joint. Before I left, Tommy told me he'd get me, whatever it took. Reach up from the grave if he had to, he said. He wasn't kidding.

So the Government moved me to a safe house in Cape Coral, at the ass end of the world. And the only thing I had to look forward to was waiting to testify at the trials of all my old friends and cooking for the Feds during our strategy sessions. I had plenty of time to experiment in the kitchen. On one rainy Saturday, I was visited by agents Larry Doss, Dick Gentlecore, and Federal Prosecutor Roma Theus, who would be prosecuting the first case. I decided to do up something extra special, just in case this was *my* last supper.

Crabmeat Appetizers

¼ pound (1 stick) butter, softened
1 jar Kraft Old English cheese
1½ teaspoons mayonnaise
½ teaspoon garlic salt
½ teaspoon Cavander's (Greek seasoning)
8 ounces crabmeat
6 English muffins (12 halves, toasted)

Melt butter in pan. (Do not burn!) Stir in rest of ingredients (excluding muffins), being careful not to overmix and break up crabmeat too much. Spread mixture generously over English muffins and bake in preheated 350-degree oven approximately 5 to 8 minutes. Broil for a few seconds to brown tops, cut into quarters, and serve. *Makes 48.*

"Great crab puffs, they got a nice bite to them," said Roma Theus, opening up his briefcase. "Now, Joe, here's a list of all the shylock payments you made to Tommy A. during the investigation. You have to study them and try to remember them. Dates, places, and amounts. You're going to be asked about them on the stand."

I rolled my eyes at these guys. My brain ain't built for that kind of thing.

"You can do it, Joe," piped up Larry Doss. "Pay attention to Roma here. He's the real deal. Graduate of Harvard, Phi Beta Kappa, number three in his class. He's intelligent, Joe, and he's going to help you."

"Gee, Larry, that's terrific, Roma being all those things," I said. "But, hey, my father was a bookmaker, and you don't hear me bragging about it." Then I went into the kitchen to cook the steaks.

Steaks Cognac

4 filets mignons, 8 ounces each
3 tablespoons olive oil (extra-virgin or virgin preferred)
2 onions, chopped
8 large mushrooms, cleaned and sliced
½ cup beef stock
¼ cup cognac (Rémy Martin preferred)
Salt and pepper to taste

*S*auté steaks to desired doneness in olive oil. Remove from frying pan and set aside. Add onions and mushrooms to steak drippings (add a little more olive oil, if needed). Sauté until almost done, approximately 8 to 10 minutes, then add beef stock, cognac, and salt and pepper to taste. Ignite to cook off alcohol. Simmer until mixture is reduced to half. Reheat steaks in sauce and serve with vegetables and baked potato. (*Note:* Asparagus Hollandaise, on page 47, also goes well with this dish.) *Serves 4.*

After dinner, Larry Doss made sure I had four or five scotches in me before he broke the news. I thought everybody was being just a little too nice.

"Joe, we got a problem," the agent began. "Indictments were handed up in New York this week, and it looks like there was a leak. We went to pick up Fat Andy, but he hasn't been home in days. His crew was scattered, too. It gets worse, Joe, and I know you're not going to like this. Tommy Agro's blown New York. He's in the wind. And we have no idea where he's hiding."

Menu

Minestrone

PORT CHARLOTTE, FLORIDA, 1985
ANOTHER FBI SAFE HOUSE

PEOPLE PRESENT:
Joe Dogs
Larry Doss
Peter Outerbridge (Federal Prosecutor)

*A*gent Larry Doss flew through the door of the safe house just as I was convincing this little babydoll waitress I'd met the night before to come and visit me. Peter Outerbridge, a Federal Prosecutor, was right behind him.

"Break out the Dewar's, Joe," Doss cried. "We nailed Tommy Agro in Montreal. You have to see that dumb little midget. He grew a mustache and thought no one would recognize him. The Royal Canadian Mounted Police picked him up for us."

"But how'd you get him back in the country?" I asked. "Ain't there a lot of red tape about crossing borders?"

"Plenty," said Doss. "Let's just say we cut a few corners and he was walked over the bridge—and into our waiting arms—up in Niagara Falls. Peter here's ready to bring him to trial."

This was the best news I'd heard in a long time, and it called for a special feast. Unfortunately, I hadn't planned on cooking. But there was enough stuff laying around the apartment for me to throw together a delicious minestrone

Minestrone

¼ cup olive oil (extra-virgin or virgin preferred)
2 to 3 cloves garlic, smashed and chopped fine
1 onion, chopped fine
½ cup sliced mushrooms
4 cups finely chopped fresh tomatoes (or 1 16-ounce can
    crushed tomatoes with juice; or 1 6-ounce can
    tomato paste with 3 cups vegetable stock)
½ cup chopped Italian (flat-leaf) parsley
2 bay leaves
1 teaspoon crushed dried oregano
2 teaspoons basil (preferably fresh, chopped)
½ teaspoon dried rosemary
1 cup precooked or canned beans (kidney, garbanzo,
    lima, pinto, or any combination of those. Note:
    garbanzo and kidney make a good combo!)
½ cup pasta (elbows, small shells, or broken spaghetti)
1 cup chopped celery
2 carrots, chopped
1 large potato, peeled and diced
1 green pepper, seeded and chopped
1 large zucchini, chopped
¾ cup green beans
10 to 12 broccoli florets

¼ cup fresh peas (or ½ package frozen peas)
¼ cup fresh corn kernels (or ½ package frozen corn)
1 small bunch fresh escarole, chopped
1½ quarts cooking water, approximately
Freshly grated Parmesan cheese
Salt and pepper to taste

*S*auté garlic, onion, and mushrooms in oil until soft (add mushrooms last, as they cook quicker). Add tomatoes or tomato paste and stock, parsley and seasonings and simmer for approximately 30 minutes. Add beans and pasta, and continue simmering. In another pot, cook (or steam) chopped vegetables in ½ cup water until nearly done, approximately 5 to 7 minutes. Combine all vegetables, including cooking water, with soup. Add additional 1½ quarts cooking water. Add escarole 5 to 10 minutes before serving (escarole cooks very quickly and will reduce to a fraction of its original volume). Sprinkle each serving with Parmesan cheese. Serve with a good crusty bread and many Dewar's if your chief antagonist on the face of the earth has just been arrested. *Serves 8 or more.*

Between 1982 and 1991 I testified in twelve trials in Florida and New York, putting away many of the guys I worked with in the Mafia. It was Tommy Agro's turn to come to court in Florida in 1986 on charges of loansharking, extortion, and attempted murder, and the judge kept yelling at me for smiling at him throughout the whole trial. T.A. was sentenced to fifteen years, but he was let out early to go home and die of lung cancer, which he did, in June of '87. As for the other guys who accompanied T.A. to my beating, Paulie Principe was acquitted by the jury and Frank Russo was indicted but never arrested.

Since then, I have been asked by several people, mostly Feds, if, knowing what I know now, I'd ever do it again. It's a tough question. Some nights, after sitting in that witness stand putting my old pals away, I went back to my room and cried. It was never my intention to break everybody, to _____ everything up.

I only wanted revenge. Revenge on T.A. and, later, on his *compare* Joe N. Gallo. Well, I got my revenge. Gallo was sentenced to ten years. T.A. died. And now I'm stuck in the Witness Protection Program, being taken to dinner out in the middle of wahoo land by U.S. Marshals in joints that advertise "Italian Night" and then serve _____ing macaroni and ketchup instead of pasta. I guess it serves me right. *Capisci?*

Cooking on the Lam

Recipes

Introduction

I'm still cooking, because I like to cook! No longer for the Mob, though. But who cares? The attorney general says that cooking for the Mob could be hazardous to my health, anyway. I got most of my old pals off the street and put them in the slammer. They were very pissed off at me. Some people just don't have a sense of humor. I guess they can't take a joke. So I took my cooking attributes on the road with me and cooked for some quite well-to-do, classy people—including some very pretty ladies.

In my escapades throughout this period of my life, I was tracked down by the Mob and they almost ended my cooking career—not to mention my life. It was close, but once again, they missed. I must be a cat. They do have nine lives, don't they? I wonder how many I have left. It's starting to look like I'm going to die of old age. Hopefully, anyway.

I kinda miss my old friends though, especially T.A. He would say to me, "Hey, Joey. Make somethin' for us to eat."

"Whaddaya want me to cook?" I'd ask.

"Make that whaddaya-call-it—ya know, that dish where you told me that guys from the north part of Italy stole that rare pig from the Japanese and they put it together with another pig and they, you know, had more pigs, or whatever! The pig with the peaches or pineapples or some kinda f____ kin' fruit that youse put on it."

"You mean Mandarin Pork Roast?" I said with a chuckle. "And it was stolen by the Italians from China, not Japan."

Me being one step up from the least mentally challenged of this bunch of guys, I used to tell them all kinds of stories to make them think they were eating something from the old country. Once they tasted it, they believed me, because, with the entrée, I'd give them a small bowl of extra-virgin olive oil and some crusty Italian bread for dipping.

The toughest time I ever had with the guys was convincing them that Lobster Thermidor was a Sicilian dish. The story I told them was that a live Maine lobster left Maine on a cold March day and headed out to sea. It swam and crawled across oceans and continents until it fell, exhausted, in Palermo, Sicily, on the last of May. The lobster was found by an old Sicilian woman who brought it home and put the poor crustacean in a barrel of cold seawater, where it began to spawn, and the lobsters multiplied. I told them mental giants that that's how we obtained Memorial Day. One of the guys said, "Jeez! Joey, it's a good thing the lobster didn't fly. We wouldn't have that holiday if she did!"

"Go figure," I said quietly to myself.

I had a lot of fun cooking for this group. But, hey! Come on, now! At least I sent 'em to the can nice and fat! *Capisci?* But, to be candid, they didn't really believe the lobster story—*some* of them didn't, anyway—but they *did* know that it was a Sicilian dish, because whenever I cooked this culinary delight, I'd serve a small bowl of tomato sauce to the side of the Thermidor.

After I was almost finished testifying at the Mafia trials, I went out on the road and traveled a lot. I had to, so I could stay at least one step ahead of the Mob. Here I was, being an honest guy trying to grind out a living, and these guys were trying to whack me. Well, I was almost honest, anyway. I just did a couple of extortions and other minor things, nothing much to speak of. Hey, I had to live, didn't I? I also met a lot of nice people as I moved around and cooked for most of them as a way of selling myself to them for friendship. Four or five times a year I hired out to cook for small parties. I'd make them a meal to die for, then wind up being the entertainment for the evening.

Here's how it went. I'd be flown into whatever city it was in and be the only person there who knew who I really was, except for the proprietors of the house or the people who were giving the gig. These well-to-do people would be multimillionaires, so you can imagine the beautiful homes they had. They were doctors and lawyers—all professional guys with lovely wives in the thirty- and forty-ish age groups.

I would be in their kitchen preparing hors d'oeuvres and the entrée, and the guests would arrive. They'd begin having cocktails and eating the hors d'oeuvres. The host would slip an A&E Network tape of me and John Gotti on *American Justice* into the VCR and the diners would watch it, not knowing that it was me in the kitchen. Just as the tape was winding down to its conclusion, I would walk into the room wearing my chef's uniform and hat and say something like, "Hey, folks. How do youse like the food so far?"

Heads would turn upon hearing a Brooklyn accent, and they'd all say, "Hey, it's him! It's 'Joe Dogs'!" They'd start giggling, and some of the ladies would grab their purses, like I was going to steal 'em or something. They loved it, and to be honest, so did I. I'd spend hours answering their questions and telling stories, and I was always paid very handsomely for my culinary efforts.

One party I cooked for stands out in my mind. The host was a prominent criminal lawyer and had his own big firm. The guests consisted of two circuit court judges, a criminal justice judge, and the attorney general of that state and their wives. We went through the same ritual as at all the other parties. Then, as they were eating their dessert, which was Zabaglione, the wife of one of the judges asked for my recipe for Blue Cheese Dressing. I told her that I'd gladly mail her the recipes for the whole dinner if she'd give me an address to send them to. The judge's wife said she would prefer that I e-mail them to her. The judge in turn said, "Maybe Joe doesn't know how to operate a computer for e-mail, so don't embarrass him."

"Oh, Your Honor, I know all about computers," I said. "I hijacked truckloads of them in my time!"

So, you see, the recipes in this book have been tasted by some very important people. Some were Mafia wise guys with big bellies, and many others were the rich, the beautiful, and the famous.

A couple of the recipes came from friends, and a couple came from great chefs. Try them, you'll love them. I know that all the people I've cooked for over the years do, and they'd welcome me back into their homes at any time for another party.

Mangia! Buon appetito!

—Joe Dogs

I t was late 1983 when I first started going to a club called Night Life, on the west coast of Florida. It was a nightclub-restaurant sort of place. The type of joint that a person of my character would hang out in and call his home away from home. It had that kind of atmosphere. I was hiding out from the Mob, waiting to go to trial against them, so I was supposed to be nice and quiet.

"Don't let anyone know who you are and where you're from, Joe. In fact, just keep your mouth shut! Try not to speak at all." The FBI agent said it with a smirk on his face. Yeah, I was supposed to be quiet, but you know what happens when you put a kid in a room full of toys and candy and you tell him not to touch anything or don't eat the candy. . . . Naturally!

So I showed a little effort and made a move on the owner of this joint and it capitalized. Irving, the owner, was paying me rent, so to speak, as we say in New York. His rent for my presence was to be $25,000 a year, to be paid at intervals of three months. Irving had already paid me my first installment and the second was due shortly. For these monies I was to see that no riffraff created any problems at the club. If a problem occurred while I was out of town, then it was to be handled when I was around. Quiet. Lowkey? Well, it's all how you looked at it. My biggest problem that I could foresee was keeping the Feds from finding out, which I later saw as no problem at all.

That's where I met Belinda, the exotically beautiful bartender. She told me that Irving wanted to know if I had a recipe for a good Italian tomato sauce, and if I did, would I be kind enough to give it to him. "Sure, honey," I said, "I'll let you have it."

I mean, like, I was shaking the guy down for about $500 a

week. The least I could do was to try and help him improve some of his food. Not that it was that bad. It was nightclub food. You know, like quick stuff made to order. Things like that.

"Tell him this is an old family recipe and not to give it out to anyone. Make him understand that I said it's a 'recipe to die for' and he'll guard it with his life, worrying that his eternal ending might be near, should anyone get hold of it," I said to Belinda, laughing.

Tomato Sauce

¼ cup olive oil (extra-virgin preferred)

3 or 4 cloves garlic, crushed and finely chopped

1 small shallot, finely chopped

1 (28-ounce) can whole peeled tomatoes (fine-quality Italian plum preferred), chopped, with liquid reserved

6 leaves fresh basil, chopped

¼ teaspoon freshly ground pepper

6 ounces pork, boned; or 1 pound Italian sausage

6 ounces beef, whole; or meatballs (see recipe, page 188)

1 (28-ounce) can chicken stock or broth (approximately)

1 (6-ounce) can tomato paste

⅓ teaspoon dry mustard

1 tablespoon dried crushed sweet basil

1 teaspoon Accent (optional)

*I*n a large saucepan heat olive oil and sauté garlic and shallot until limber (about 1 or 2 minutes); don't brown. Add chopped tomatoes without juice from the can (set juice aside) and cook for 10 minutes, stirring occasionally. Add fresh basil, pepper, and the juice from the can of tomatoes and stir. Cook for an additional 10 minutes, then stir again while adding the meats and two-thirds of the stock to the saucepan. Cook until it comes to the boil, then add the tomato paste, mustard, basil, and Accent and stir until well blended. Cook, covered, for 3 to 4 more hours at a simmer, stirring occasionally and adding more chicken stock if sauce gets too thick.

Skim grease from the top of sauce as it's cooking. Note: In this recipe there is no salt needed.

If Italian sausage is used, par-cook it on a flat pan in a 350°F oven with ⅛ inch of water on the bottom of pan. Bake for 30 minutes. It will finish cooking when added to the sauce. For meatballs, follow the same procedure. Discard the pork and beef, if using, at the end of the cooking time. *Makes 4 cups sauce.*

In April 1984 I was finally going on the first trial. I was as nervous as a snake in a belt factory. I had totally lost my appetite, but the FBI agents who were baby-sitting me didn't. They were famished. I mean, like they always wanted to eat and drink. Hey! Why not? The government picked up the tab.

"Hey, Dogs, what's for dinner? I'm hungry as hell," Agent Doss said. "Why don't you make a nice appetizer, and I'll order a pizza for tonight. Just tell me what to pick up at the store." Agents Richard Bennett and Gunnar Askland were also guarding me that evening.

After giving Agent Larry Doss a grocery list, I took a short nap, only to dream that the Mob caught up with me and was roasting me on a large skewer. I wondered how I tasted. I had hoped they got indigestion, or, as we say with the Italian tongue, *agita*.

Stuffed Mushrooms

1 8-ounce can lump crabmeat
1 pound medium-size mushroom caps
¼ cup olive oil (extra-virgin preferred)
2 cloves garlic, crushed and finely chopped
1 small shallot, minced
½ red bell pepper, seeded and cut in fine dice
¼ pound (1 stick) butter, melted
Juice of ½ lemon
Salt and black pepper to taste
1 sleeve Ritz crackers, crushed into fine crumbs
Heavy cream to taste (if needed)
¼ cup water (approximately)
¼ cup dry white wine
¼ cup chopped Italian (flat-leaf) parsley
¼ cup freshly grated Parmesan cheese

$\mathcal{P}$lace crabmeat in large bowl and break it up into small pieces with the back of a fork. Set aside. Clean mushroom caps and set aside. Heat olive oil in a saucepan and sauté garlic, shallot, and red bell pepper on low heat until nice and soft, about 10 minutes. Add mixture to bowl containing crabmeat. Into same bowl add melted butter (make sure it's not too hot; just warm), lemon juice, and salt and pepper, and mix thoroughly. Mixture should be wet and loose. Add Ritz cracker crumbs and mix in well. If mixture is too dry, add heavy cream until you get the right consistency.

Fill cavities of mushroom caps generously with crabmeat mixture. Place caps in layers on a flat-rimmed microwavable dish. Fill dish with ⅛ inch water and microwave for 2 minutes on high. Let cool for 5 minutes, then drain water from dish and replace with wine. Microwave for an additional 90 seconds. Remove caps from microwave dish and place in 1 layer on regular baking sheet. Sprinkle parsley and Parmesan cheese on caps and broil in preheated oven for 1 or 2 minutes, until golden brown. *Makes 12 to 15 pieces.*

CRAB CAKES

$\mathcal{U}$se the same basic mixture of ingredients (eliminate mushroom caps, olive oil, water, wine, parsley, and Parmesan cheese). To the basic crabmeat mixture, add 1 large egg, beaten, combine well with mixture, then form into individual cakes. Roll each cake in pulverized Ritz cracker crumbs until well coated. Heat equal amounts of butter and olive oil in a frying pan, and sauté crab cakes on all sides just until nicely browned. *Makes 4 individual cakes.*

It was my first day as a witness for the government. I was getting ready to testify against my cohorts—guys that I did shakedowns with, gang-related things, and many other criminal activities. Was I sorry or in remorse for what I was doing by testifying against them? No, I wasn't. The Mob had traveled from New York to Florida to come down and kill me. There were two tough hoods with Agro who ambushed me and beat me to a pulp. They left me for dead. No, I wasn't sorry. I wasn't afraid, either. Although apprehensive, it was *my* turn to get even.

As I entered the courtroom, I glanced over at the defendants. They glared at me. The judge, a man named Alcee Hastings, said loudly, "Mr. Iannuzzi, after the bailiff swears you in, give the court reporter your full name and spell out your last name. Please speak loud enough so that the jury can hear you."

As I was doing as ordered, I looked at the defendants. They were seated very close to me on the right. All of them had smirks on their faces. One of them was giving me the finger. Intimidated I could not be. Not at this point. On trial this day were: Robert "Skinny Bobby" DeSimone, Paul Principe, Salvatore Reale, Ronald "Ronnie Stone" Pearlman, and John "JJ" DeNoia.

My attention wandered over to the prosecutor's table, and FBI Agent Larry Doss and Prosecutor Roma Theus gave me the thumbs-up sign. I made a promise to myself that if all went well this day, I would cook them a nice dinner that evening.

I glanced over at the guilty parties one more time to see if they still were smiling. They were. I was in for a long day.

Shrimp Scampi Gourmet-Style

2 pounds large shrimp (under 20 per pound)
¼ pound (1 stick) butter
3 cloves garlic, crushed and minced
1 medium shallot, finely chopped
¼ teaspoon black pepper
½ teaspoon Accent
¼ cup heavy cream
2 tablespoons chopped Italian (flat-leaf) parsley

*R*inse, shell, devein, and butterfly shrimp. Set aside. In a large saucepan melt butter over low heat until bubbling (do not let it turn brown and burn). Add garlic and shallot to pan and sauté for about 3 minutes, or until limber. Add shrimp to pan and cook on both sides until pink all over, about 4 minutes. When shrimp are done, remove from pan and set aside. Quickly add pepper, Accent, and cream to saucepan and stir vigorously. Put shrimp back in pan and stir into sauce mixture.

Pour shrimp with sauce mixture onto a warm serving platter. Sprinkle chopped parsley over everything and serve immediately with rice or noodles. *Serves 6.*

The trial was in its third week and I was still under direct examination. I'll say one thing about the government's prosecutors. They are thorough. The defense attorneys were sharpening their knives waiting for my return.

I went to the Night Life that evening to see Belinda. Irving came up to me and handed me an envelope and said, "Here's your second installment—$6,250, correct?"

I looked at him and then darted my eyes around the room to see if I was being set up, but everything looked kosher. If anything, I learned to be extremely careful while working with the FBI. "Yeah, thanks, Irv," I said, then changed the subject.

Belinda came running over, kissing me, saying how much she'd missed me. I asked her if, when she got through working, she would come to my apartment, and I would fix her something to eat. She gave me a coy smile and said, "Is that all?" I smiled back and said we'd have something light.

I left the club around ten that night and went to my place to prepare the snack I had in mind. It was a good thing I did some food shopping after getting off the plane.

Marinated Asparagus Wrapped with Prosciutto

24 thin asparagus spears
¼ cup olive oil (extra-virgin preferred)
Juice of ½ lemon

2 cloves garlic, minced
1 tablespoon capers
Pinch of dried crushed thyme
Salt and black pepper to taste
¼ pound prosciutto, thinly sliced

*B*lanch asparagus spears; drain, cool, and place in large, deep dish. Combine all the rest of the ingredients, except the prosciutto, and pour over asparagus. Marinate in refrigerator for 3 to 4 hours. Remove asparagus from marinade. Wrap prosciutto slices around asparagus and place on serving platter. Drizzle marinade over all. Serve chilled with Italian bread and dry red wine. *Serves 4.*

Belinda came over at two-thirty A.M. We ate, drank some wine, and talked.

"That was a nice light snack, Joe. Who gave you that recipe?"

"Some guy from Chicago. His name is Oniello. We did a couple of burgs together."

"What's a burg?"

"A burglary—you know, a robbery, a B&E, breaking and entering, like being a crook. That's how I used to be. I'm honest now."

Belinda spent the weekend with me. She left her daughter with a neighbor sitter. We had a good time, but she started to ask too many questions about my flying out after every weekend.

"Belinda, look, baby, you know I won't answer your questions, so why are you so persistent? I'm working on a business deal. I told you that. So please try to accept my word," I said with exasperation. There was no way I was going to tell this baby doll anything.

"Hey, Joe, I know we're not supposed to discuss the case, but stop f____ around on the witness stand. You 'looked like you were unbelievable,' " the FBI agent said to me.

"Listen, Larry, it's no picnic sitting on the f____ witness stand answering questions all day long. The jury is bored to hell with us as it is. At least once in a while they're able to giggle or crack a smile while I'm sitting on the witness stand. Anyway, I'm on cross-examination now and you're not allowed to talk to me about anything pertaining to the case. So shudup!" I ended, smiling at him.

Agent "Tricks" Tierney, agreeing with me, said, "Yeah, Larry, shut up and let Dogs get started."

"I'm going to cook something nice for you guys tonight," I said. "We'll go out to eat tomorrow. I'm tired of eating all that garbage in those restaurants we go to. I'm glad you guys got this apartment to stay in."

"Okay, Dogs, enough bullshit. Start cooking, I'm starved," Agent Askland said. The guys had picked up the groceries that I gave them a list for. So I was all set.

Chicken Cordon Bleu

4 chicken cutlets, pounded thin
1 tablespoon unsalted butter, melted
2 thin slices boiled or baked ham, cut in half
2 thin slices Swiss cheese, cut in half
2 tablespoons all-purpose flour

½ teaspoon freshly ground black pepper
1 tablespoon unsalted butter
2 shallots, minced
¼ cup white wine (sherry) or chicken stock
½ cup heavy cream
¼ teaspoon dried crushed oregano
Capers (optional; see Note)

*P*lace chicken cutlets on large dish and brush all over with melted butter. Place 1 slice of ham and cheese on top of each cutlet. Roll up each cutlet like a jelly roll and tie well at each end with butcher's string. In another dish, mix together flour and pepper. Toss and roll cutlets gently in mixture to coat; shake off excess. In a nonstick skillet, melt butter on medium heat. Add shallots and sauté for 2 minutes, stirring constantly to prevent scorching. Add cutlets to skillet and sauté approximately 4 minutes total, turning them occasionally until they are golden in color. Remove cutlets and set aside. Add wine and reduce slightly, then add cream and stir, while bringing slowly to the boil. Put cutlets back into sauce, increase heat, and bring to the boil again. Add oregano and reduce heat. Let mixture simmer until chicken is cooked and sauce is slightly thickened (approximately 10 to 12 minutes). Remove cutlets from skillet and place on warm serving platter; cut away all string. Pour sauce over cutlets and serve immediately. Buttered rice goes well with this dish. *Serves 4.*

Note: If sauce gets too thick, add chicken stock gradually. On the other hand, if you need to thicken sauce a little more, add some more butter while sautéing. A few capers may be added for a tart-like taste.

Cross-examination was tough. Mark Krasnow was an extremely tough attorney. The defense was riding my ass so much that I felt I needed Vaseline or some other ointment to relieve the pain on my bottom. He said things like "You're lying, aren't you, Mr. Iannuzzi? Even Judge Hastings called you an unadulterated liar. You put my client Bobby DeSimone at a meeting that never existed. You're a low-down liar and an actor. These people didn't try to kill you. Someone else did. Didn't they, Mr. Witness?"

I hated being called Mr. Witness, so I had to retaliate. "You're wrong, Mr. Shyster. They came there to Don's Italian Pizza, beat me with a bat and a pipe, and left me for dead."

Krasnow hated being called that name. "Objection, Your Honor! Will you please admonish the witness? I want to be addressed by my surname!" Krasnow screamed.

"Mr. Iannuzzi, will you please stop calling Mr. Krasnow names and agree to his request? I'd like to get over with this trial before Thanksgiving. I know we're only in the latter part of May, but we're moving at a turtle's pace. Continue, Mr. Krasnow."

I think the judge was really biased against me and he didn't care who knew it. Sometime later Congress impeached him. That's how it went all day long—Krasnow calling me Mr. Witness, and me calling him derogatory lawyer names. Objections all over the place all day from the defense and the prosecutors. It was very tiring.

"Irving, the veal piccata you serve here doesn't really taste that good. Who do you have cooking in the kitchen? Must be a new guy."

"Yeah, Joe, the other guy quit. He opened his own business. I don't know what the hell I'm going to do. Do you have any suggestions?" Irving said with pleading eyes.

I felt sorry for the guy, so I said, "I'll tell you what I'll do, Irv. When Belinda comes to my place tonight, I'll give her a recipe for that veal dish and you tell your new cook that's the way you want it prepared. I really don't want to get involved in your business affairs. I'm not your partner, you know, not to that extent anyway."

"Yeah, you're right, Joe," Irv said. "I'm sorry. I didn't mean to impose on you, but I would appreciate that recipe. That other cook was good, you know. He was with me for a long time."

As Irving was talking, two unruly-looking guys walked into the place and ordered a drink from Belinda, who was tending bar that night. Their vocabulary was abusive, and Irving's eyes looked at me. Well, he was paying me to keep control, so . . .

"Irv," I asked, "are these guys members? I don't remember seeing them here before."

"No, I would never allow trash to be members here," Irv replied. "Do me a favor and get rid of them for me, please? I'd rather not call the police."

When Irving made the statement "I'd rather not call the police," a light bulb went on in my head. I thought to myself: Could it be that Irving hired these two guys to come in here, thinking I would back off and he would get out of his obligation with me? Well, if he did, he was going to be one sorry night club owner.

I excused myself, went quickly to my car and put on my lead leather gloves with cut-off fingers, and put my snub .38 in my waistband under my jacket. I went back inside, walked up behind the guys, and slammed my hands over their backs, which I'm sure jarred them, and said, "Fellas, that's no way to order a drink, now, is it!" I reached between them and grabbed the two bottles of beer off the counter before they knew what was happening.

"Hey, you m____! What did you do that for? Who the f____ are you? Who do you think you're f____ with?" the one on the left said, as the guy on the right took a half-assed swing at me.

I stepped back, taking a glancing blow under my eye on the right cheekbone. I slammed the guy on my left in the face with one of the beer bottles, knocking him off the stool. And then I quickly turned to my right to position myself. Clenching my fist, I hit the other guy so hard in the jaw you could hear the crunch. He was out cold, but the guy I hit with the bottle was getting to his feet. I gave him a drop-kick to his head, which made him plead for no more. I looked at Irving. He was staring with his mouth open, like he didn't believe what had happened.

"I think you should call the cops, Irv, so this crap won't come in here again. Where the hell did they come from, anyway?" I asked, thinking that Irving was going to squirm out of this one. To my surprise, he went right over to the phone and did what I suggested. I left just before the police arrived, as Irving knew I couldn't get involved with the police.

When Belinda came to the apartment that night, later than usual, she gave me the rundown on what had happened. I was wrong about Irving.

"When the police arrived, Irving told them how the bad guys were conducting themselves and that they became very ungentleman-like, so a man who was contemplating joining the club defended the bartender from injury. The cops asked what the gentleman's name was. And Irv said all he knew him by was his first name, which was Frank, but if he decided to join the club he would give the police his full name. How's your eye? Here, let me put an ice pack on it so it doesn't swell up." I smiled at her and gave her a big hug. Then I prepared a veal piccata dish.

❧

Veal Piccata

1 pound veal, cut scallopini-style
All-purpose flour for dredging
6 tablespoons butter
½ cup dry white (sherry) wine
¾ cup heavy cream
Salt and white pepper to taste
1 teaspoon Accent
Butter for thickening sauce
Lemon juice (approximately 1 tablespoon per serving)
Capers (5 to 6 per serving)

With a mallet, pound veal slices very thin, or have butcher do it. Dredge veal in flour and shake off excess. In a sauté pan, melt half the butter. Place veal in melted butter and sauté for 1 to 2 minutes on each side. Remove veal from pan and set aside on a warm platter. Raise heat and add wine. It will ignite. Let flame burn out, then add cream, salt, pepper, Accent, and remainder of butter. Stir and reduce by half. Put lemon juice in pan, add veal back to mixture, and let simmer for an additional 2 minutes, stirring again. Add capers and serve. To thicken sauce, add some more butter. Serve with linguine or asparagus with hollandaise sauce. *Serves 4.*

Back in the courtroom I was being mocked by the defense attorneys about the black eye that I had. One of them said something like, "What happened to your eye, Mr. Iannuzzi? Did the Mafia beat you up over the weekend? Did you tell the FBI about it, and did they come to your aid?" he continued to mock.

"Objection, Your Honor. The witness's eye has nothing to do with this case. If it did, then I would have brought it up before the court." That was the prosecutor, Roma Theus.

"Sustained!" cried the court. "By the way, Mr. Iannuzzi, what *did* happen to your eye? You don't have to tell me if you don't want to, but it would relieve everyone's mind in the courtroom along with mine if you did."

"It's really not a big deal, Your Honor," I said. "I was out with this hooker over the weekend, and when I went to approach her she slugged me in the eye and told me, 'Uh-uh! Not on the first date.' "

The jury got a good laugh from that, and even the judge smiled and asked defense counsel, "Well, are you satisfied with that answer? Continue with your cross."

The rest of the day was brutal. They reamed my ass good and hard, and it was a relief to go and cook for the three agents who were baby-sitting me.

"Hey, R.B., did you get the stuff from the grocery store?" I asked.

"Yeah, Dogs, I got it, and I got a can of Alpo for *you* to eat. You know, you really look like a dog—a really ugly one," Agent Richard Bennett said.

Shrimp Creole

1½ pounds medium shrimp (25 to 30 per pound)
4 tablespoons vegetable oil
1 heaping tablespoon butter or margarine
5 or 6 tiny hot chili peppers, cut in half
1 green bell pepper, seeded and diced
1 red bell pepper, seeded and diced
1 large Vidalia onion, diced
1 pound mushrooms, cleaned and sliced
3 or 4 stalks celery, diced
2 or 3 cloves garlic, crushed and finely chopped
2 tablespoons cornmeal
1 14½-ounce can cut tomatoes (Hunt's brand preferred)
Chicken stock (approximately 26 ounces)
⅓ teaspoon freshly ground pepper

*R*inse, shell, and devein shrimp. Set aside.
In a saucepan over medium heat, add oil and butter together and bring almost to bubbling. Add all ingredients from hot peppers through garlic and stir well, tossing the veggies. Add the cornmeal and mix everything together well. Cook until vegetables are translucent, about 5 minutes. Add the canned tomatoes, stir well, then add most of chicken stock. Let simmer for at least 30 more minutes, adding pepper and remainder of stock as, and if, needed. Just before sauce is finished cooking, add shrimp

and cook for 4 or 5 minutes—no longer! Stir slowly but constantly. Serve over rice. *Serves 4.*

Note: Do not cook shrimp more than 4 or 5 minutes! They will get stringy and tough.

Belinda had taken the weekend off, so she and I had a couple of days together. I was gone from Fort Myers for two weeks this time. The agents couldn't fly me back from Miami. The trial was winding down, and I had about one more week of cross-examination and that was it. Thank God! I was exhausted. While I spent some time with Belinda, I showed her how to make a couple of desserts that I had picked up in my travels.

Semifreddo (Italian Ice)

½ cup sweet white wine
½ cup sugar
½ cup water
½ cup lemon juice, freshly squeezed
1 large egg white, room temperature

Add wine, water, and sugar to saucepan and cook over medium heat until sugar is dissolved and syrup just starts to boil. Cover saucepan, raise heat to high, and boil 1 minute. Lower heat, remove cover, and simmer 10 minutes without stirring. Remove mixture from heat and refrigerate, uncovered, until completely cooled, approximately 30 minutes. Stir lemon juice into cooled syrup, pour mixture into pan, and freeze until firm throughout but not solid, approximately 1 hour.

Beat egg white to soft peaks. Transfer lemon ice to chilled bowl and beat with a whisk until smooth. Add egg white and mix well. Return to pan, spread evenly, and freeze until very firm, at least 3 hours. *Makes 4 4-ounce cups of ice.*

Sweet Peaches with Creamy Zabaglione Topped with Crushed Amaretti (Almond Cookies)

8 medium peaches, peeled, halved, sliced ⅛-inch thick
(reserve liquid from peaches)
¼ cup plus 3 tablespoons sugar, divided
¼ cup orange liqueur
3 large egg yolks, room temperature
⅓ cup Marsala wine
1 cup heavy cream
1 tablespoon confectioners' sugar
8 Amaretti cookies, crushed

lace peach slices in large bowl. Add ¼ cup sugar and orange liqueur to coat. Toss well. Refrigerate 2 to 5 hours. In another bowl, whisk egg yolks with 3 tablespoons sugar until pale yellow, approximately 2 minutes. Add Marsala wine. Set bowl over pot of simmering water. Whisk constantly until mixture is very pale yellow and has consistency of whipped cream, approximately 8 minutes. Do not let mixture boil. Set bowl in larger bowl filled with ice water to cool.

In another bowl, whip cream and confectioners' sugar to soft peaks. Fold half the cream into the pale yellow mixture to combine. Fold balance of whipped cream into mixture.

Arrange peach slices, with their liquid, in a large bowl or individual stemmed glasses. Top with creamy zabaglione and sprinkle with crushed Amaretti cookies. *Serves 6.*

I was sitting on the lounge chair in my living room at my apartment thinking about the past six treacherous, grueling weeks that had gone by. Yes, the trial was over. In fact, it was over for me five days ago. There were three convictions out of five. De Noia was dismissed before the ending. Principe was acquitted. The three convicted were waiting to be sentenced at a later date. It had been a long trial. The prosecutor was on direct for eighteen days, and the defense was on for eleven. My ass cheeks sprouted blisters from sitting on that hard chair. When I arrived back in Fort Myers, I didn't let anyone know that I was back in town. I left my car at the airport and took a cab to the place I called home now. I unplugged my phone and just relaxed. I wasn't in the mood to see anyone. Not even Belinda. If there was something I needed, I'd send for it by taxi.

After I got the call about the convictions, the agents and the lead prosecutor called to say they wanted to come down and celebrate. "We'll go over to that place——Night Life," the prosecutor said. "I really like that place. Do you still go there once in a while, Joe?" It was a question that was saying he wanted information. He didn't like me going there because it was a New York–style club.

His question was a test. There's no way I could go in there with that group of guys now. I mean, like, the FBI agents aren't the smartest guys in the world, but they aren't the dumbest either. That's all they would have to see——the people there kissing my ring, so to speak. It would be very embarrassing for all of us. I wouldn't put them in the position where they felt that I was being underhanded to them. I liked them, and in my corrupted mind I felt that I was doing no wrong. It had nothing to do with the case we went to court on. So why not!

"Hell, no, Roma!" I said. "I haven't been to that place in a long time. Their kitchen got closed for quite a while. They were closed because of rodent infestation."

"You're kidding." Roma laughed. "I'll be damned. It looked like such a nice club, too. That's a private club, isn't it, Joe? I remember how well they treated you over there. That's the place I told you not to frequent too often. Remember?"

"Yeah, I remember. That's the place, all right." I had to make it sound more convincing, so I added, "It was in the newspaper here about what happened. One of the members took some guests there for dinner to celebrate their twenty-fifth wedding anniversary, and while they were eating, three or four rats fell on their table from the suspended ceiling and were running all around the table eating from the people's plates. Yeah, it was really bad for them. The board of health closed them down. They just now reopened, but they lost a lot of their business. I know I wouldn't even have a drink there, much less eat."

"I wouldn't either. Oh, well, you can cook, then. Whaddaya say, Joe?" Roma asked.

"Sure. Why not?"

They came down the following week. Seven of them. So I prepared lasagna for them.

Classic Meat Lasagna

This dish tastes best if it's prepared and cooked a day in advance, so all the flavors can blend really well and the mixture gets a richer taste.

Lasagna Mixture

> *2 pounds ricotta cheese*
> *1 pound mozzarella cheese, divided into 2 parts (¼ pound diced; ¾ pound sliced)*
> *3 or 4 large eggs*
> *2 tablespoons finely chopped Italian (flat-leaf) parsley*
> *½ teaspoon salt*
> *¼ teaspoon crushed black pepper*
> *2 quarts Tomato Sauce (see recipe, page 166)*

....

1 package frozen flat lasagna noodles (4 inches by 6
inches) (purchase in Italian delicatessen)
1 pound Meatballs, sliced (see following recipe)
1 pound Italian sausage links, sliced
½ pound freshly grated Parmesan cheese
¼ pound pepperoni, sliced

*T*n a large mixing bowl put ricotta cheese, diced
mozzarella, 3 eggs, parsley, salt, and pepper, and
combine thoroughly. If mixture is too thick, add other egg
and blend well. Set aside. In a 13″-by-9″-by-3″ pan, put
layer of tomato sauce to cover bottom. Place layer of noodles
on top of sauce to cover sauce completely. Spread a layer of
ricotta (about ⅓-inch thick) over noodles. On top of ricotta,
put layer of sliced meatballs and sausage. Then lay some
mozzarella and Parmesan on the top of meat. Top that off
with slices of pepperoni and healthy layer of tomato sauce.
Then start layering again, in same order: tomato sauce,
noodles, etc. Finally, top off the lasagna mixture with final
layer of noodles.

Bake, covered with foil, in a preheated 350°F oven for
1 hour. Remove from oven and let cool for at least 1 hour.

Refrigerate overnight. The next day, bake, covered, at
350°F for 45 minutes, or until piping hot. Then remove foil
and bake for an additional 15 to 20 minutes. Cut into
desired-size squares, sprinkle with Parmesan cheese, and add
a little more tomato sauce on top. *Serves 8.*

Meatballs

½ pound ground beef
½ pound ground pork (bulk skinless sausage)
⅓ cup ketchup
1 large egg
4 slices bread (soaked in water, then well squeezed)
⅛ teaspoon salt
¼ teaspoon black pepper
Bread crumbs

*P*reheat the oven to 325°F.

In a large bowl put all the ingredients together, except bread crumbs, and mix thoroughly. To get the right consistency, add the amount of bread crumbs needed to roll into balls the size of a small lemon. Bake for 30 minutes or until tender (test by jabbing a sharp knife into the center of one meatball). *Makes 12 to 16 small meatballs.*

Note: If you're going to use the meatballs to make sauce, bake them first for 30 minutes. Then add them to the sauce and let simmer in the sauce for a couple of hours.

Three months after my first trial, I was getting ready to go to my second. This time I was going against a crooked cop. He was the chief of police in Riviera Beach, Florida, and we had this guy good, because I got him on video camera, recorded telephone conversations, and Nagra body recorders.

At trial, on direct examination by his lawyers, Boone Darden acknowledged that he took money from me but he claimed he was making his own case. He said something like, "I was conducting an investigation of my own. I knew this here man, Mr. Iannuzzi—they call Joe Dogs—is crooked. Yes, sir, I didn't know Mr. Iannuzzi was working with you all. I had my own case going, I swear it." He also testified that he had put the money I had given him in his office filing cabinet. He reached into his pocket and pulled out an envelope and said, "Here it is, right here."

The trial broke for a recess. Then, upon learning that the report with the serial numbers of the bills the FBI had given to me for the bribe had been misplaced, the brilliant prosecutor, Peter Outerbridge, had some bills photocopied and left the photocopy sitting out conspicuously on his table in the courtroom for Darden to see during the break. Darden, who obviously saw the bills, must have assumed that the prosecution was about to compare serial numbers. When Darden's lawyers resumed their direct examination after the recess, they asked him if the envelope contained the same bills that I had given him.

He replied, "I can't be sure. It got commingled with some other money."

He testified that he had taken the money home when he retired and kept it in the family Bible. Darden shifted nervously in his seat. Peter Outerbridge felt sorry for him as the jury was laughing at his reasoning for taking the bribe. After a withering cross-examination, Mr. Outerbridge would not embarrass the chief any longer. I believe the jury was out for two hours before they pronounced him guilty as charged on all counts. He was sentenced to six years. He wasn't really a bad cop. He was the Mob's cop.

Back in Fort Myers I was making an Italian vegetable dish that Belinda requested.

Sicilian Caponata

¾ cup olive oil (extra-virgin preferred)
½ pound pearl onions, whole; or 2 medium onions, thinly sliced
1 teaspoon salt, plus to taste
2 red bell peppers, seeded, sliced, and diced
4 cloves garlic, minced
1 (16-ounce) can crushed tomatoes (Hunt's brand preferred)
Black pepper to taste
1 teaspoon dried crushed thyme
¼ cup chopped fresh parsley
½ cup dry white wine
6 stalks celery with leaves, thinly sliced
1½ pounds eggplant, cubed
½ cup red wine vinegar
2 tablespoons sugar (or to taste)
¼ cup capers, rinsed and drained
1 cup pimiento salad olives

*I*n a deep skillet, heat ¼ cup olive oil, then add onions and a pinch salt. Cook over low heat until onions are translucent, about 5 minutes. Add peppers and another pinch salt, cover, and cook until crisp-tender, about 5 minutes. Add garlic and cook until fragrant, about 2 minutes. Add tomatoes, 1 teaspoon salt, black pepper, thyme, parsley, and wine. Cover and simmer gently until onions and peppers are tender, about 15 minutes.

In another skillet, heat 2 tablespoons olive oil. Add celery with their leaves and cook until softened, about 5 minutes. Transfer to a bowl and season with salt and pepper. In the same skillet, heat remaining oil. Add eggplant and cook over moderate heat, tossing occasionally until lightly browned, about 3 minutes. Transfer eggplant and celery to skillet with onion-tomato mixture. Adjust seasonings. Cover and simmer gently until vegetables are cooked through, about 20 minutes.

In a bowl, combine sugar and vinegar. Stir well to dissolve sugar. Add vinegar mixture, capers, and olives to vegetable concoction and simmer over low heat to blend flavors, about 2 minutes. Transfer to a serving bowl and serve. *Makes about 1 quart.*

Note: This mixture can be stored refrigerated for two weeks, or frozen for several months.

Important: Do not overcook! Vegetables should retain their shape and texture.

It was late 1984, and Belinda and I had split up. She wanted a commitment, but there was no way I could give her one. I lived every day in deception and fear, so I advised her to move on.

"There's no future with me, Belinda," I said. "You're better off with someone else."

So she did. She moved to California, and I started to hang around another restaurant, called the Prawnbrokers. I met a lot of nice people there and started to have some fun. I was getting ready to leave the area, so I told Irving he had only one more payment to go and I would be out of his hair. He thanked me profusely for my help and said to me that if I ever needed anything just to call him.

A young lady named Lucy came over to my apartment one night when she got off work. She was a bartender at the Prawnbrokers, and she had a bag full of clams that her employer had given her. Lucy was a very pretty, petite blond lady with extremely sensual lips, and she had been to my place a few times before for a late-snack dinner. "Hey, Joe, baby," she said, "I brought some clams over. How about fixing some of them up Casino style? You know how to do that?"

"Yeah, sure, Luce," I said to her, "but, Christ, it's midnight."

"So what? Is there a f___ curfew on the f___ things? Come on, make them and I'll fix you a drink. Just make believe that I'm the other broad—what's her name . . . Beelinda?" Lucy mimicked. I forgot to mention that Lucy's beautiful sensual mouth also had a sailor's vocabulary occasionally. She was a native New Yorker who'd moved into the area to be near her parents.

"Okay, sweetheart," I answered laughingly. I'd make the clams the way a friend of mine used to make them when he worked at the Waldorf-Astoria in Manhattan.

Clams Casino

24 cherrystone clams, freshly shucked, left on half shell
¼ pound (1 stick) butter
½ cup diced green pepper
1 clove garlic, minced
½ cup onion, grated
½ cup chopped Italian (flat-leaf) parsley
1 tablespoon anchovy paste (or finely chopped fillets)
Salt and pepper to taste
3 strips bacon (approximately), cut into 1-inch squares

*P*reheat the oven to 400°F.
      Lay clams on a large baking sheet and set aside.
Melt butter in a saucepan and sauté green pepper until soft. Add garlic, onion, and parsley and sauté a little longer. Add anchovy paste (or fillets) and salt and pepper to taste and mix thoroughly.

      Spoon the sauce over the clams, and place a piece of bacon on top of each clam. Bake until bacon becomes crisp. Serve immediately. This is a great dish to serve as an appetizer. *Makes 24 pieces.*

I had gone out one evening with a date, Melanie, to a club in Fort Myers Beach to listen to this great female singer, Betty-something-or-other; anyway, she had a fantastic voice and she was a friend. The room was dark and secluded, and unless you were in the room for at least five to ten minutes, you wouldn't be able to see very much. I was dancing with my date, having a nice time, when I overheard in a hushed voice, "That guy looks like Joe Dogs."

I danced to another part of the room quickly and became apprehensive. My date noticed this and asked me what was wrong. I tried to slough it off and was trying to think of an excuse to get out of there, but it would have seemed odd, as we'd just got there thirty minutes earlier. I took a chance and asked her at the table if she would do me a favor and go to my car and get me my .38 pistol, and I told her where it was in the car.

She looked a little concerned and agreed, but asked, "Do you expect a problem? Is there something going on that I should be concerned about? Tell me, Joe, you can trust me!"

I told her that I thought I saw someone in the place who was my arch enemy and that I knew he carried a gun. I was going to excuse myself and go to the car and get my gun, but she said no need and put her hand down her skirt from the waistline and handed me a Baretta .25-caliber automatic.

"There's eight bullets in there," she said, "one in the chamber and seven in the clip. I already released the safety, so it's ready to fire if you need to. Now let's get the hell out of here and go to my place."

I looked at her, shook my head in disbelief, and smiled.

I paid the check and we left. Melanie didn't ask me one question, except how to cook this certain dish, so I complied (in her kitchen, of course).

Pizzaiola Sauce

3 tablespoons olive oil (extra-virgin preferred)
2 cloves garlic, minced
1 (16-ounce) can whole peeled tomatoes (fine-quality
*   Italian plum preferred), crushed*
¼ teaspoon salt
¼ teaspoon black pepper
½ teaspoon dried crushed oregano
1 tablespoon chopped Italian (flat-leaf) parsley
Chicken stock (if needed)

Heat oil in a skillet, then brown garlic (do not burn!). Add tomatoes, salt, and pepper and cook over medium heat for about 15 minutes. Add oregano and parsley, and let simmer for another 5 minutes. Add some chicken stock if mixture becomes too thick. Serve over steak, chicken, or fish. *Makes 1 cup sauce.*

"Show me how to make that rice the way you Sicilians make it. Please?" Melanie asked.

"This isn't a Sicilian dish. They make this all over Europe, I think, and it's really good."

❧

Risotto Milanese

6 to 7 cups rich chicken stock
4 tablespoons butter, divided
1 large onion, finely chopped
2 cups Italian rice
        (Arborio preferred)
½ cup dry sherry
½ teaspoon salt
¼ teaspoon black pepper
¼ teaspoon saffron threads, crumbled
⅓ cup freshly grated Parmesan cheese (or to taste)

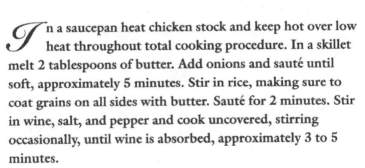

*I*n a saucepan heat chicken stock and keep hot over low heat throughout total cooking procedure. In a skillet melt 2 tablespoons of butter. Add onions and sauté until soft, approximately 5 minutes. Stir in rice, making sure to coat grains on all sides with butter. Sauté for 2 minutes. Stir in wine, salt, and pepper and cook uncovered, stirring occasionally, until wine is absorbed, approximately 3 to 5 minutes.

Start adding stock to rice mixture ½ cup at a time until each is absorbed. Repeat the process until 2 cups stock have

been added. (Be sure to maintain the mixture at a simmer.)
Stir frequently. Add crumbled saffron to rice; cook until
absorbed. Continue adding stock, ½ cup at a time, until
rice is tender but *al dente*, approximately 20 minutes.
Remove saucepan from heat and stir remaining
2 tablespoons butter, plus cheese, into mixture, combining
well. Risotto should have a creamy consistency. Serve the
dish immediately; risotto doesn't keep that well. *Serves 4.*

I had contacted the FBI and told them of the incident that had
happened at the nightclub in Fort Myers Beach. Larry Doss had
previously told me that the Mob had put the word out to look for
me and that there was a big price on my head. I was waiting for
word from the FBI about when they were going to move me.

Larry Doss contacted me a couple of days later. "Sorry, Joe,
but headquarters in Washington refused to move you. They said
that you're not supposed to be bouncing around in nightclubs.
Look at it from their perspective, Joe. If you didn't go to that
place, then you wouldn't have been recognized. That's how they
look at it," the agent said.

"Hey, Larry, what are they—f____ nuts, or what? What am I
supposed to do, stay home and play with myself?"

"That's just what you're supposed to do as far as they're concerned. I'm sorry, there's nothing I can do."

I got in a big argument with him over the phone and all, but it
wasn't his fault. I was the moron. I should've told them that I was
recognized while I was food shopping or going to the post office or
something of that nature. Yes, I was the jackass for telling them the

truth. No problem; I had Irving's money. It's a good thing that I wasn't so kosher with the FBI. I'd be up shit's creek without a paddle now, because for me to move, it takes three months' rent (first, last, and security deposit), and you have to find a decent rental where they have security. My place has to be thoroughly furnished, as I didn't have any furniture. Deposits for a phone, electric, gas, new groceries—everything. Because when I moved, no one knew I was leaving. This was the new life I had to live, and to this day it's still the same.

I had moved north of Fort Myers about forty miles up the road into a little town called Punta Gorda. The place I rented was very secure. There was a guard at the main entrance to the gated community at all times, and they also patrolled around the whole area at night. My rent was $850 a month. The rental office told me that I needed references, so I put $2,550 cash on the table and asked them if they would like to have a couple of more months' rent in advance; they told me that my reference rating was extremely sufficient. I don't want to seem redundant but, like I said, thank God for my earning ability and for Irving.

It didn't take me long to find myself another baby doll. I met this young good-looker at a Ramada Inn lounge. Her name was Lorretta with two r's. Instant love! Again! Only this one was a great cook, and immaculate in the house, as was that baby-doll Lucy from Fort Myers. The third time I saw Lorretta, I wanted to show off some of my culinary tricks. I told her I was going to fry her some chicken, and she said, "Step aside, sonny, and let a Polish girl show you how to make that dish." And she did. I mean, this lady could cook. I watched her!

Simple Fried Chicken

1 2 ½- to 3-pound fryer chicken
2 large eggs
¼ cup milk
1 heaping tablespoon mayonnaise (Hellmann's brand preferred)
Flour for dredging, seasoned with salt and pepper to taste
1½ cups plain dry bread crumbs
4 tablespoons vegetable oil
2 tablespoons butter
½ cup chicken stock

Cut chicken into 6 pieces (2 legs, 2 thighs, and 2 breast halves) and remove all skin. Make egg wash by combining eggs, milk, and mayonnaise; mix well. Get each piece of chicken good and wet in the egg wash. Roll chicken in seasoned flour, shake off excess, then dip chicken back in egg wash, and finally roll into bread crumbs. Make sure chicken is completely coated.

In a large frying pan, heat oil and butter, then chicken over medium heat, cooking on all sides until nicely browned, approximately 15 minutes. Remove chicken and place on warm plate. With a wooden spoon scrape all browned bits from pan into a bowl or any nonplastic container and set aside. (These drippings may be used to make gravy.) Place chicken back in pan and pour in stock. Cover pan and steam chicken for 15 to 20 minutes over very low heat. *Serves 3.*

I missed the people that I had become friendly with in Fort Myers, and I also missed my income. Irving gave me an additional payment for my outstanding service. At least this is what I told myself. And I really believed it. I was pretty flush at the time. Cash-wise, that is. Although I made a donation every four months to a needy organization and I gave Belinda $1,200, every time I received a payment I still had enough for a good time. It wasn't like I kept it all for myself. I shared whatever I could with others. It made me feel like that guy Robin Hood. Him being some kind of a hood made me wonder if Robin was from the Gambinos.

I had been living in this apartment for about six or seven months now, and I left my place to drive to the grocery store. As I drove through the security gate, I noticed a late-model car across the street parked on the embankment. As I made a right turn, I saw his headlights go on. The car pulled right behind me and was following me. I pulled into a parking lot where this large grocery store was and went inside and got a shopping cart. I pushed the cart behind one of the aisles and waited to see if anyone who looked familiar or suspicious came into the store. I watched for about five minutes, then started to shop. I thought to myself that I could have been mistaken. I had my gun with me and I carried it always, ever since that incident at the club in Fort Myers Beach. I was paranoid a lot since then, so I was very careful. When I checked out, I asked the cashier for an extra bag, and I was leaving with my groceries and I held the gun inside the bag, just in case someone tried to surprise me: then I would be able to defend myself. They didn't, but that same car was behind me again, and soon after I pulled out of that parking lot. I went through the security gate, and in my rearview mirror I noticed that the car went back to its same position on the lawn across the way.

I was on the phone immediately, talking to the guard at the gate, asking him if he knew who was in the car across the street from him. He told me it was a private investigator. He also told me that someone else had called the police, and the police questioned him, and he had to show his ID. The police told the guard that the man was within his rights because it was private property. I called up Larry and informed him about what happened and he said to get out of the area quickly. I was hungry, so I made myself a quick cup of coffee and I ate some leftover cheesecake that I had made.

Cheesecake

Cookie Crust

> *1 cup all-purpose flour, sifted*
> *¼ cup sugar*
> *1 egg, beaten*
> *½ cup butter, softened*
> *½ teaspoon vanilla extract*

Preheat the oven to 400°F. Combine all ingredients and mix thoroughly. Put the whole mixture into a pie pan. Flatten out and pat into pan. Bake for 10 minutes, then allow to cool.

FILLING

1¼ pounds (2½ 8-ounce packages) cream cheese
4 teaspoons flour
¾ cup sugar
¾ teaspoon vanilla extract
2 tablespoons sour cream
2 tablespoons milk
4 egg yolks, room temperature

*P*reheat the oven to 500°F.
    With an electric mixer set to medium, beat cheese until soft; add flour and sugar while beating until blended; add vanilla, sour cream, and milk and blend thoroughly; add egg yolks, 1 at a time, beating each well as you put it in. Pour mixture into cookie crust. Bake for 6 minutes. Lower heat to 200°F and bake for 30 minutes more. *Do not overbake.* Cool on wire rack, then refrigerate. Leave in pan until well chilled. *Serves 8.*

I took the FBI agent's advice and quickly packed some clothes. Enough to disappear with. I planned to return a week later to get the balance of my stuff, or whatever a carload could carry. I knew that I would have to leave my exercise machine behind, as it was too big and too heavy to lug by myself. These are the perilous ways I had to live. When I started to leave, I thought that I had no real destination to go to. Before Lorretta and I had split up, I remembered her saying that she was in Savannah, Georgia, one time and how much she liked it. We split up because the FBI figured I should tell her my status with them, and she handled it for a while because she was Polish, but even her nationality couldn't block the element of fear, so she hit the road.

"Savannah? Why not?" I said to myself.

As I drove through the gate I made a left and, sure enough, old hound dog pulled right behind me once again. I thought that this moron was so obvious that he was a joke. I wanted to go north on Route I-75, so instead I went south, figuring that I would somehow lose this guy. I was riding on the highway for a few miles, and when I approached the very first exit I came to, I signaled to get off. It was three A.M., so it was deserted outside. No traffic whatsoever. As I was exiting, the other car was tailgating me. I stopped the car on the ramp and put my emergency flashers on. I opened my window and waved my left arm in a circular movement for him to come over to the car, as there wasn't room for the other car to pass. My .38 was on the seat, and now in my hand. I was told that he was a PI, so there wasn't that much to worry about. The moron started walking over, and his hands were clean, as I noticed in my rearview mirror. I jumped out of the car in a flash, gun in hand,

and grabbed the guy by the hair and slammed him against my car, then down to the pavement. The guy was whimpering, not knowing what was going to happen to him.

"What are you following me for, you _____ so-and-so?" I blurted out. I went on and on for about five minutes with him lying on his back down on the ground, and every so often I'd smack him.

He showed me his ID and told me that he was trailing another man and he made a mistake. I let him get up and I told him that he was a liar and that he wasn't believable. I was screaming at him and pointing the gun at his head. As he was backing away, he turned and started running down the ramp onto a highway. I fired three shots high in the air and went to his car and took his keys from the ignition, put them in my pocket, and left.

I drove south for two exits, then turned around and headed north toward I-10 to I-95. As I was passing the area where the incident had occurred, I noticed the PI walking back toward his vehicle.

"What do you mean, headquarters turned me down for the moving expenses? You're the one that advised me to leave. Did you tell them that?"

"Yes, Joe, I told them, and they said that the case was costing the government too much money already. There's nothing I can do," Larry Doss said.

"Well, my friend, there's something that I can do. Tell those empty suits in Washington that I said to go f____ themselves. I quit," I said, hanging up the phone.

That's par for the course. That's how it had been all the while I was working for the FBI. It wasn't the field agents; it was the moron agents in Washington. They didn't know their ass from their elbow about what was going on. If they don't want to keep their word, then I'll walk. The agency in New York would suffer.

It didn't take me long to find a new baby doll. She was gorgeous, a double for Morgan Fairchild. Naturally, I showed her one of my attributes and cooked her a nice Italian dinner before I gave her the salami. Daffney worked as a manicurist in a beauty salon, and when I went in to get my nails done it was instant love.

Daffney moved in, bag and baggage. I had rented an apartment in a little town offshore from the beach on Tybee Island, in Savannah, Georgia. The apartment was nicely furnished. The kitchen was well stocked with pots, pans, and dishes.

Shrimp alla Pizzaiola

12 jumbo shrimp
Pizzaiola sauce (see recipe, page 195)
¼ cup freshly grated Parmesan cheese
¼ cup mozzarella cheese, grated

*P*reheat the oven to 375°F.
Rinse, shell, devein, and butterfly shrimp. Place shrimp, tails up, in baking dish. Top with pizzaiola sauce, then sprinkle Parmesan cheese over all. Bake until almost cooked through, approximately 6 minutes. Top with mozzarella cheese. Place under broiler until mozzarella is cooked through and lightly browned. Serve immediately. This dish is nice served with rice or pasta. *Serves 4.*

It was about three weeks before I heard from the FBI. A New York agent by the name of Richard Tofani flew down to talk to me. I'd advised him that I had already quit, and there was no way I was going to trial in New York anyway. I went to pick him up at the airport, and off the plane, last, comes this tall, good-looking Italian guy about six-foot-four. Tofani and I hit it off real well. He told me that the New York office would reimburse me for whatever money I laid out and proceeded to convince me, without threats, to continue to go on to trial. I agreed mainly because they had just caught Thomas Agro. He had been a fugitive from the get-go. He was the one I really wanted. The others convicted themselves, more or less.

Richard stayed at my apartment for the length of his stay in the Savannah area. I had a two-bedroom town house.

One night we went out to one of the clubs and took four ladies back to my place. Tofani had been bragging about how I made baked stuffed clams, so the girls volunteered to buy all the groceries that we needed if I would cook for them. I agreed because my chick, Daffney, was staying at her mother's while Tofani was in town. At least, that's what she told me. Oh, don't misunderstand me now. Daffney wasn't one to fool around. She was a gal who only bothered with one party. I just happened to be a Democrat.

∽∾

Baked Stuffed Clams

4 dozen cherrystone clams, freshly shucked, left on half shell
1 package frozen chopped spinach
1 package frozen chopped kale
¾ cup (1½ sticks) butter
1 cup plain dry bread crumbs
½ cup freshly grated Parmesan cheese
1 tablespoon anchovy paste (or finely chopped fillets)
3 tablespoons chopped Italian (flat-leaf) parsley
2 tablespoons Worcestershire sauce
½ cup Madeira wine
Salt and freshly ground pepper to taste
½ pound bacon
½ tablespoon Tabasco sauce (approximately)

*L*ay clams on a very large baking sheet and set aside.
In a saucepan, steam spinach and kale in 1 cup water until soft. Drain off water and pat vegetables on paper towels to remove any excess water. Return to pot and add butter and melt it. Add all other ingredients except bacon and Tabasco sauce, and stir briefly to combine. Put mixture in a blender and almost purée it. Set aside.

Preheat the broiler.

In a skillet, fry half the bacon until well done, then crumble it and stir into blended mixture.

Run clams under broiler for 1 or 2 minutes, just until they are half-cooked. Remove clams from broiler and cover each clam with a 1-inch square piece of uncooked bacon. Put clams back under broiler for about 1 minute more. Then cover each clam generously with spinach-kale mixture, and pat mixture lightly to make sure it will stay in place. Splash a little Tabasco sauce on top of each clam. Bake clams in a 375°F oven for 10 to 12 minutes. Serve hot as an appetizer. *Makes 48 pieces.*

I was on trial in Miami. This time it was for Tommy "T. A." Agro and Andrew "Fat Andy" Ruggiano. This was the trial that I was waiting for. Not so much for Fat Andy, but for that low-life Agro. I had nothing against Ruggiano. His cohorts hung him with all their blabbering over the telephone. That's what made him do fourteen years in prison. He should have never gone away. His own Mafia family put him in the can. Agro showed up in a wheel-chair—another sympathy tool the mobsters use. DeSimone came to his trial wearing a neck brace, but the jury read his scam and convicted him anyway.

I looked over at Agro and gave him a pearly-white smile. He immediately snarled at me, which made me smile even more. I had tape-recorded him so many times that I myself couldn't believe it. What really got him was when I wore the body recorder to all those meetings in New York City with him blabbing away, getting all his cohorts convicted.

Yes, I smiled at him so much that my face hurt at day's end. There were a couple of wise guys seated in the courtroom, besides others such as private investigators and New York attorneys. Why those attorneys were here watching me testify, I didn't know. I told the FBI that I would testify only in the Florida trials and that I wouldn't go to New York. They had agreed with me, so there was reason for me to doubt them or to have concern.

This trial went on for fifteen days on my testimony itself. The case seemed open and shut to the agents and the prosecutors. I could taste victory before I even finished with my testimony. So I had some agents over and I cooked a real treat as the wine and Scotch were being poured freely. We were in for a big night, with me doing all the cooking.

Sauerbraten with Potato Dumplings and Red Cabbage and Apples

To make this great-tasting, long-cooking meat dish, use either cross-rib, top sirloin, or bottom round. The meat needs to have some fat on it.

MARINATING MEAT

4 to 6 pounds beef
1 cup cider vinegar
1 cup wine vinegar or claret
2 cups water
2 onions, sliced
2 tablespoons sugar
12 cloves
6 bay leaves
6 whole peppercorns
2 tablespoons salt
½ lemon, sliced

To marinate meat prior to cooking, take a crock pot or large glass bowl and place meat in it. Pour in half of each of the liquids, or enough to cover the meat, which might take more than half the liquids; however, use equal amounts of the liquids. Add all other ingredients and leave meat in this mixture, refrigerated, for at least 2 days (depending on amount of meat used). Turn meat over

in marinade once or twice a day. Keep meat covered
with a tight-fitting lid during entire marination
process.

COOKING MEAT

> *Butter, beef drippings, or suet*
> *Reserved meat marinade*
> *1 cup crumbled gingersnaps (about 6)*
> *¾ cup flour*
> *Vegetable or beef stock, if needed*

*U*se dutch oven or roasting pot with a tight-fitting lid,
large enough to accommodate meat.

Take meat out of marinating liquid and let drain.
Reserve marinade. Pat meat dry with paper towels.

Place in the cooking pot one of the following: butter,
beef drippings, or suet (just enough to brown meat on all
sides, approximately 3 tablespoons fat). On medium to high
heat, melt fat until it sizzles. Place meat in fat and brown
well. Gradually add all reserved marinade, including all
spices, then add crumbled gingersnaps. Cover. Allow meat
to simmer slowly for 2 to 3 hours, depending on its size.

Just before meat is done, on a pie pan place ¾ cup flour,
distributed evenly. Run under broiler until brown. Add to pot
with meat, and stir in quickly, cook for 10 minutes to thicken
gravy. If gravy gets too thick, add a little vegetable or beef
stock. After cooking 10 minutes, remove meat from pot and
strain gravy. Place meat back in pot with strained gravy and

cook 5 minutes longer. Remove meat from pot, slice, place on warm serving platter, and pour gravy over it. *Serves 8 to 10.*

POTATO DUMPLINGS (*KARTOFFELKLÖSSE*)

> *6 medium potatoes*
> *2 teaspoons salt*
> *2 eggs*
> *¾ cup flour*
> *½ cup bread cubes*
> *¼ teaspoon nutmeg*
> *1 teaspoon sugar*
> *1 teaspoon farina*

*B*oil potatoes in their jackets. When cooked, remove skins and put through sieve or ricer. Spread on a clean towel for 1 hour to dry out moisture. Place potatoes in a large bowl and sprinkle 2 level teaspoons of salt over all. Make a hollow in middle of potatoes and break two eggs into it. Stir in flour, bread cubes, nutmeg, sugar, and farina. Work this all in together until no more sticks to your hands. If mixture is too wet, add a little more flour and a few extra bread cubes.

Roll this mixture into small balls and then drop into boiling salted water. After potato balls come to surface, let them boil for about 12 to 15 minutes. To test for doneness, take one ball out and cut through it. When cooked, center should be dry, not soggy. (You must be careful not to boil too long because potato balls will fall apart or become wet and soggy.) Remove all potato balls from water with a slotted spoon. Once they are removed from the boiling water, place them on a hot, lightly buttered platter. When ready to serve, pour the gravy over them or pass it separately. *Serves 8 to 10 as a side dish.*

RED CABBAGE AND APPLES

> ¼ cup butter or margarine
> 2 medium apples, peeled, cored, and thinly sliced
> 1 medium onion, diced
> 1 medium head red cabbage, cored and shredded
> 1 cup water
> ½ cup red-wine vinegar
> ⅓ cup sugar
> 1½ teaspoons salt
> Pepper to taste
> 1 dried bay leaf

*I*n a 4-quart saucepan over medium heat, heat butter or margarine until hot but not burning. Add apples and onion and cook until tender, about 10 minutes. Add cabbage, water, red-wine vinegar, sugar, salt, a pinch of pepper, and bay leaf and heat mixture to boiling. Reduce heat to low; cover and simmer about 40 minutes stirring occasionally, or until cabbage is very tender. Discard bay leaf before serving. *Serves 8 to 10 as a side dish.*

I was on the witness stand for two more days. When I was leaving the seat that I'd occupied for fifteen days, I looked at Agro and blew him a kiss good-bye and said something out of earshot of everyone else. The judge yelled at me over the defense's objections. I didn't care. I smiled anyway. While the agents were driving, I noticed they were doing an awful lot of talking on the radios. There were also four cars full of agents, when normally there were two. I was concerned, naturally.

"What's up, Larry? Why all the cars?" I asked.

It took him a moment to answer me, and then he said, "Eh, we want to get you safely on the plane, Joe. You did a great job, by the way."

I noticed that we were going through a gate where there were three guys with rifles, and I saw that they were waving all four cars through. I knew they were FBI agents outside there and we were driving onto the tarmac at a clandestine airport.

"Hey, Larry!" I shouted. "What the f____ is going on here? This ain't the airport that I fly out of."

Everyone was quiet. Then Larry said, "I didn't want to tell you this, Joe, but the Mob is watching for you at every airport, so I Teletyped headquarters and told them of the urgency to get you out of here and how it was an emergency to see that you arrive safely and all, so Webster sent his own private jet to fly you there."

Wow! I thought. The boss of the FBI is really concerned. I mean, like, come on now, I really gotta be somebody. I'll tell you the truth, it felt nice. It really felt good. "But what about my clothes?" I asked. "What are you gonna do? Mail them to me?"

"We already packed them for you, Joe. You're all set," Larry Doss said.

They rushed me onto the Lear jet. Agent Rich Tofani was on the plane. That was odd. Tofani put a Scotch-on-ice in my hand as the plane took off.

"It won't take us long to get to Savannah in this thing, will it, Rich?" I observed. I noticed a look of surprise on his face.

"Savannah? Didn't Doss tell you that you had to testify in the Colombo trial in Manhattan? I swear to God, Joe, he told me you knew and that you agreed."

I was silent. I didn't say a word. I just kept staring at Richie. I didn't believe what had happened. I wasn't mad. I had been had. It was my own fault for trusting them. Tofani was probably a part of this conspiracy. I laughed. "So then all this bullshit about the airports being watched is really all bullshit, huh?"

"No, it's not, Joe. You're a hot ticket. I saw the Teletype Larry sent, and that's the only way we could have gotten Webster's jet and his pilot. Didn't you see all the agents with guns? They were ready for war. Don't worry Joe, we're well equipped to take care of you in New York," he added. "There won't be any f___ups here."

When we landed I was half bombed. There was a slew of agents at this clandestine airstrip, too. "Oh, well . . . ," I said as I departed from the plane.

The Colombo trial in Manhattan was exasperating for me. I was extremely tired, getting off one witness stand and onto another in a different state against a different Mob family. It was exhausting. There were twelve defendants on trial. Carmine

"Snake" Persico was one of the defendants, "Little Dom" Cataldo, who at one time was my real close friend and *compare* (before he put out a contract on my life), was also there, plus the under-boss captains and a slew of soldiers—or wise guys, as I would refer to them. The year was 1985. While I was on the witness stand, reputed Mob boss Paul Castellano of the Gambino family was gunned down in front of Spark's steakhouse on Manhattan's east side. I don't know if that was what caused a defense attorney to become ill, but the judge gave the defense a ten-day time-off period for that attorney to get well before the trial started again. I welcomed the delay. I couldn't wait to return to the Savannah area. Thank God the piles on that defense attorney's ass had burst.

I was at my apartment on Tybee Island again when I received a call from a gentleman named John Andronokis. He owned a jewelry repair shop in the Oglethorpe Mall in Savannah. He and I became friendly, and although I had ulterior motives—because, as always, I was looking to make some money the easy way—I proposed an illegal scam to John, thinking he would jump at the chance.

He said, "Joey, my friend, I came to this wonderful country when I was a boy, and I love the American way. I would never do anything dishonest for any reason. I make a nice living now, but there were times I was in bad shape—real bad shape. So, Joey, I have to say no to you."

I admired the guy for his honesty, and he and I became good friends. John came from the countryside in Greece. He was a big, muscular man with that handsome European look. His wife, Betty Jo, was a darling pretty southern lady. The reason for the call was that John had invited me to the house that he built in Blairsville,

Georgia, which was in the Blue Ridge Mountains. I desperately needed a rest, so this was a godsend. We met, and the three of us, with me riding in the backseat, drove up to the mountains. He had a beautiful house with a lake close by, so I relaxed with a fishing pole in my hand.

My stay there was nice, and while I was there, I prepared a dish for John and Betty Jo.

Béarnaise Sauce

2 tablespoons red-wine vinegar
1 small shallot, finely minced
1½ teaspoons dried crushed tarragon
4 egg yolks
Pinch black pepper
½ cup (1 stick) butter, melted and kept hot
1 teaspoon parsley, minced

Boil vinegar and reduce by half. In a blender on high speed, put reduced vinegar, shallot, tarragon, egg yolks, and black pepper and blend for 1 minute. With blender still on, slowly add bubbly hot butter through blender-cap opening in a steady, slow stream. Make sure not to let any water from hot butter get into sauce. Blend for 30 seconds. Place sauce in gravy boat and stir in parsley. Serve this great, rich sauce with some favorite steak dishes (see recipes, pages 104 and 150). *Makes ½ cup sauce.*

When I returned to New York to resume testifying, I was well rested and tough on the defense attorneys. It was my third day back and the Snake's lawyer asked me in open court but out of the jury's presence if I would meet with him and his client alone in the judge's chambers. I was surprised. I was lost for words. I didn't know how to answer because we had never talked about anything like this while we were practicing. I looked around the courtroom to see if I could get some sort of clue from one of the three prosecutors, but they didn't show any emotion or anything. I didn't even want to be at this trial. I had nothing against the Colombo family. Their big mouths, talking on the phone, had got them into this jam. I really didn't want to be here, but I had no choice. They made the evidence, and I was here to attest to it. Everyone's eyes in the courtroom were on me, and it was so quiet you could hear a fish fart.

The court said, "Mr. Iannuzzi, you're allowed to meet with the defense if you want. Nothing will happen to you. That I can guarantee. If you choose not to, it's all right also. It's your decision. No one can force you."

I looked at the Honorable Judge John F. Keenan and said, "No, Your Honor, I don't wish to!" With that statement, I noticed a sigh of relief come from the prosecution. Apparently I had made the right decision.

The day ended, and on the way back to Governors Island, the agents took me to an army PX store and we did some shopping. I bought some nice veal chops and prepared them a northern Italian way, with a spaghetti dish.

Veal Chops Milanese

4 large veal chops, sliced 1 inch thick
Salt and pepper to taste
Flour for dredging
1 large egg, well beaten
1 cup plain dry bread crumbs
2 cups seasoned bread crumbs
4 tablespoons butter
1 lemon, sliced in wedges

Sprinkle veal chops with salt and pepper. Flour chops on all sides; then shake off excess. Dip chops into egg, then coat well with bread crumbs. In a sauté pan, melt the butter until bubbling. Sauté chops slowly on both sides for a total of about 8 minutes. Place chops on a warm serving platter and pour butter from pan over them. Serve with lemon wedges. *Serves 4.*

Spaghetti with Garlic and Olive Oil

4 quarts cold water
4 tablespoons salt
1 pound spaghetti or linguine
½ cup plus 2 tablespoons olive oil, divided
    (extra-virgin preferred)
6 cloves garlic, finely chopped
2 tablespoons heavy cream
Freshly ground black pepper, to taste
Freshly grated Romano or Parmesan cheese (to taste)

Fill a large stock pot with cold water, add salt, and bring to the boil. Add spaghetti, let water come back to a rolling boil, and cook until *al dente*, or approximately 8 minutes. Drain and let stand in pot. Add ¼ cup olive oil to pasta and toss around, preventing strands from sticking together.

In a large pan add rest of olive oil and sauté garlic until slightly golden in color. Add heavy cream, whisk in well, then place spaghetti in pan. Sprinkle black pepper over pasta. Toss pasta around until all of it is coated with the sauce. Place on a warm platter, sprinkle grated cheese all over, and serve immediately. *Serves 4.*

That trial ended about a month later. The jury was in deliberations for almost a week. All parties were found guilty and sentenced to a zillion years. I know the Colombo boss, Snake, received sixty-five years from this trial. He later got sentenced to one hundred years in the commission trial. My good close friend Dominick "Little Dom" Cataldo, the one that put a contract out on my life, got thirty-five years. He died in prison a couple of years later. All of the defendants got hit heavily with the sentences.

It was 1987, and once again I had quit the FBI because they cut my salary again and the government didn't give me what was promised me by the agents. I held out until I was compensated. I had to fight for everything. This was the Gambino trial in Brooklyn, New York, where I was to meet the extremely tough attorney Mark Krasnow for the fifth and, unfortunately, last time. On trial at this time was the under-boss, Joe "Piney" Armone, and the *consigliere*, Joseph N. Gallo, of the Gambino LCN organized-crime family. Both were found guilty and sentenced heavily.

After that, Mark disappeared under strange circumstances. I sure hope Mr. Krasnow doesn't sleep with the fishes.

After the trial we celebrated, and guess who cooked. If you said Joe Dogs, you were right. I made them a New England boiled dinner and German potato salad. This corned beef recipe is dynamite. It was given to me by some chick named Carol, a real beautiful-looking sensuous baby doll who lived in Stuart, Florida. We were very close friends.

Corned Beef and Cabbage

5-pound boneless brisket ("1st cut"—flat half—preferred)
2 or 3 cloves garlic, peeled and left whole
2 dried bay leaves
½ teaspoon black peppercorns, left whole
1 medium head cabbage
12 to 18 small carrots
12 to 18 small red potatoes

Place meat in a large dutch oven along with garlic, bay leaves, and peppercorns; add just enough water to cover. Bring to the boil, then reduce heat to low. Cover tightly and simmer for at least 3 hours, or until fork-tender. Remove meat and keep warm. Cut cabbage in wedges and add pieces to cooking liquid in dutch oven, along with carrots and potatoes. Cook vegetables until fork-tender. Slice beef and arrange around a platter along with the vegetables. *Serves 8 to 10.*

Fagioli with Fresh Sage

1 pound white navy beans
1 large onion, sliced
2 dried bay leaves
2 large branches fresh rosemary
3 cloves garlic, minced
1 cup dry white wine

Chicken stock
Salt and pepper to taste

*R*inse beans well under cold running water. Soak in water overnight in refrigerator, making sure beans are covered with water.

Place beans in pot over low heat and simmer, adding onion, bay leaves, rosemary, garlic, and wine. Continue to simmer, stirring occasionally from bottom of pot upward, making sure beans don't stick to pot. Simmer until beans are firm but tender, approximately 1 hour. As liquid reduces, keep adding chicken stock. When beans are done, place in warm bowl, remove rosemary sprigs and bay leaves, and add salt and pepper to taste. *Serves 4.*

German Potato Salad

3 pounds medium potatoes (about 10)
6 slices bacon
1 tablespoon flour
½ cup red-wine vinegar
⅓ cup water
⅛ teaspoon black pepper
2 teaspoons sugar
1 medium onion, thinly sliced or chopped
¼ cup chopped green pepper
Chopped parsley for garnish

$\mathcal{I}$n a medium saucepan, boil potatoes in their jackets until fork-tender. Cool and remove skins. Slice and set aside.

In a large skillet, over medium heat, cook bacon until crisp and remove to paper towels to drain. Add flour to bacon drippings and whisk well. Cook for 5 minutes, then add vinegar, water, pepper, and sugar and whisk together. Next, add onions and green pepper, combining well with mixture. Simmer for 5 minutes.

Chop bacon and add to potatoes. Pour mixture from skillet over potatoes and sprinkle with chopped parsley. Serve warm. *Serves 8 to 10.*

Carol's Chocolate Cake

CAKE

½ cup vegetable shortening

1½ cups sugar

2 eggs, room temperature

1 teaspoon vanilla extract

2 ounces (2 squares) baking chocolate, melted

2 cups cake flour (or 1¾ cups regular flour), sifted

½ teaspoon salt

1 cup buttermilk

1 teaspoon baking soda

1 tablespoon vinegar

*P*reheat the oven to 350°F.

Using an electric beater, cream shortening and sugar until fluffy. Add 1 egg at a time, beating well. Add vanilla and chocolate; mix well. Add sifted flour, then salt, alternately with buttermilk. In a small bowl, dissolve baking soda in vinegar. When bubbly, add to batter and mix well.

Pour batter into greased 9-by-13-inch pan(s). Bake for 35 to 40 minutes, or until a toothpick inserted into cake comes out dry and clean.

Note: Cool cake 10 minutes before removing from pans.

FROSTING

¾ cup sugar
1 egg, room temperature
¾ cup milk
3 tablespoons flour
½ cup vegetable shortening
½ cup margarine or butter
½ cup confectioners' sugar
1 teaspoon vanilla extract

*I*n a saucepan over medium heat, whisk together all ingredients. Cook until thickened and bubbly, stirring constantly. Remove from heat and cool thoroughly. When cool, transfer to large bowl of an electric mixer and add shortening, margarine, confectioner's sugar, and vanilla. Beat on high speed for 5 to 7 minutes, or until mixture gets to spreading consistency.

Frost the cake. You can garnish the top of the cake with chocolate curls. *Serves 8.*

Note: In humid weather you may have to add more confectioners' sugar.

Also in 1987, the FBI got me an additional lump sum of money, and I was supposed to be all finished testifying for them. I purchased a small fried-chicken take-out joint in Georgia. It employed four women, all of them country cooks, and real wonderful people. It was a business that I probably would still own today if it wasn't for the FBI lousing it all up for me. I didn't know the first thing about country cooking. I didn't have to. The ladies that I had there knew it all. They were the best. The girls did everything. We served a buffet-style lunch, and it was what the average working stiff could afford. Of course, I was an outsider, and if I was still there today, which is fourteen years later, I'd still be one.

The Brooklyn FBI agents and Prosecutor Peter Lieb said they needed me for a trial that made me wind up in the hospital with a T.I.A. I wound up having to abandon the business. Then Judge Shirley Wohl Kram postponed the trial from a Thursday to the next Tuesday. She said, "I have business tomorrow on another trial. Then the weekend we are off."

My country help thought that I had abandoned them, because I wasn't there to pay them on time and to greet them every day. I had one of the girls pay everybody cash out of the receipts, but that wasn't good enough. They wanted their Mr. Joe. Country people are very funny. They don't want to feel insecure. I even paid them better than the previous owner, but when I didn't show up the day that I told them I would be back, they took off and went to work for my competitor. When I returned, I found the place very clean with all the equipment and furnishings intact, but no employees. All the help had left me, and no one else in town would work for the New York Yankee. I stayed for a week trying and even practically begging people to come and work at the Chicken Delight, but it was no use.

I deserted the place. I lost $40,000. The FBI giveth, and the FBI taketh away. I went home and cooked dinner for this nice lady that I met on the plane flying back from New York. She was a beautiful Spaniard.

Red Snapper en Papillote

½ *cup milk*
1 *teaspoon dried crushed oregano*
1 *pound red snapper fillets (2 pieces)*
¼ *cup olive oil (extra-virgin preferred)*
½ *medium onion, sliced*
2 *tomatoes, chopped*
1 *clove garlic, minced*
1 *teaspoon capers*
8 *small pitted black olives*
¼ *cup dry white wine*
Juice of ½ lemon

1 teaspoon salt
⅛ teaspoon freshly ground black pepper
Papillote bags (purchase in specialty supermarket)

*I*n a deep glass or ceramic dish, mix together milk and oregano. Add snapper, cover, and marinate in refrigerator for at least 45 minutes.

In a frying pan, heat olive oil and sauté onion until tender. Add all other ingredients to pan, except snapper, and simmer, uncovered, for about 20 minutes, or until sauce is thickened.

Preheat the oven to 350°F.

Remove snapper from marinade, place on paper towels, and pat dry. Put each piece of fish in a paper (*papillote*) bag. Spoon half the sauce over each piece of fish. Seal paper cooking bags securely, put them on an ungreased pan, and bake for 20 to 25 minutes. Slit bags open carefully so the steam inside doesn't hit you in the face. Put fillets on plates and serve with lemon wedges. *Serves 2.*

Losing so much money in that restaurant ownership really put a crimp in my pocket, or more like a cramp. I had to do something quick. I sat down and put my criminal mind together. I tried to be an honest citizen, but the good guys stuck it right up my ass. I was happy pulling down $800 to a grand a week, and it would only have gotten better if the Feds would have left me alone.

I took a ride to an exclusive resort area in the South, checked into a hotel, and in the local newspaper I scanned the rental ads in the classified section. There were some pretty juicy looking ads in there. I came up with a rental that looked very feasible and made an appointment with a Mrs. Cotton, the wife of an engineer. The rental was on the ocean, and the rent was $1,800 a month with a two-year lease.

I went out and bought a cheap typewriter, and on one of the three blank phony driver's licenses I typed in the name "Gordon Roughly." I did the same thing to a blank Social Security card and a birth certificate, because I might have needed additional ID. I made like I was from Salt Lake City, Utah, and I was in this resort spot looking for a decent rental, as my plans were to move into the state permanently, and this resort looked like a nice area. I told Mrs. Cotton that my wife and three children were getting anxious to move and be with their dad. I added, "We also have a ten-year-old Yorkshire terrier that is part of our family, along with a cat and a canary. I hope you understand that without the animals I can't even think of renting the place."

She said she was happy to hear about the animals and that the engineer said the decision was hers on how to pick a tenant. I told Mrs. Cotton that this was by far the best rental I had seen, and at a very reasonable price. The lady said that they most likely could get a bit more for the rental, but that they—her and her husband—decided to rent it to someone who was willing to take a lease for two years and could naturally afford it. She wanted two months' rent and a month's security deposit in advance, plus a $2,500 security deposit for the animals. This was very reasonable, but I didn't have it. I quibbled with her for a while, telling her that the $5,400 rental deposit was agreeable, but I couldn't see why she wanted so much security deposit for a Yorkie that was housebroken and a cat that was declawed.

"We're not pigs, Mrs. Cotton," I said. "I'll be only too happy to have you meet my family. We're going to put our house up for sale, so there's no rental references that I can give you."

I bluffed, laying $5,400 in cash on the table, hoping she'd go for it. She did. I'd like to think it was my charm and charisma that made her change her mind, but money does funny things to people when seen in a lump sum.

"Will cash do? I haven't had time to start a checking account yet," I said. I had given her a few phony references that I made solid beforehand, and I believe she checked them when she excused herself for about ten minutes.

With the lease now in my name, I started to go to work at my scam. It was two weeks afterward that the lady and her husband left for Europe, and I had lain around the pool and beach long enough. First, I advertised in three out-of-state newspapers for the rental. Then I went to the fishing pier with a camera and paid a deep-sea fisherman $20 to take a few pictures of me with the sailfish that he'd caught. Then I hired a freelance photographer to take some professional pictures of the place: the inside of the house, including the bedrooms, dining area, living room, kitchen, and even the laundry room. Outdoors there was the tennis court, pool, and the view of the beach and ocean. I was making a brochure of the place, and the picture with me and the fish was a big seller for the rental. The ad that I placed stated all the amenities plus the rent, which was $2,500 a month. It also advertised that the rental was for three months and listed the good engineer's phone number to call, as his wife had let the phone stay in their name, along with the rest of the utilities. That alone saved me quite a bit of money for deposits. I used another set of identifications and gave myself the good engineer's name. I nosed around his place, where their personal papers were, and found something with his Social Security number on it.

So that was legitimate. This had to be done correct, in case one of the prospective renters was smart enough to check the utility companies or wanted to see my identification: then I could produce one.

I rented the place to nine different people. They all gave me different deposits, which I required, at least $2,500 in advance. One person gave me $10,000 for the three months and the security. I was adamant that they give me a cashier's check, which wasn't a problem. These I could get cashed very easily at any check joint for a small percent of the juice. All in all, after taking all the expenses that I'd laid out, I profiled $27,500. *Bunko.*

The last person to give me a deposit was a pretty lady named Barbara from Oklahoma City. She was very friendly, so I invited her to stay for dinner and overnight as I wanted to show her one of my attributes. She stayed a week. The first night we had:

Linguine with White Clam Sauce

⅓ cup olive oil (extra-virgin preferred)

2 tablespoons butter

3 cloves garlic, minced

1 small shallot, minced

½ cup dry white wine

12 cherrystone clams, shucked; juice reserved

½ tablespoon lemon juice

1 teaspoon dried crushed oregano
Pinch salt and pepper
½ pound linguine
2 tablespoons lemon rind, grated and minced (see Note)
2 tablespoons chopped Italian (flat-leaf) parsley

*I*n a saucepan, heat oil and butter and sauté garlic and shallot until limber. Add wine and cook until alcohol evaporates, about 1 or 2 minutes. Add reserved clam juice, lemon, oregano, salt, and pepper. Bring to the boil and cook until liquid is reduced by half.

Meanwhile, you should have your linguine boiling in a pot of salted water. It needs to cook for about 8 minutes. When done, drain pasta but do not rinse. Return to cooking pot and keep hot.

Lower heat under clam mixture, then add clams and lemon rind. Add drained linguine to saucepan and toss thoroughly. Place on a warm platter and sprinkle parsley over top. *Serves 2.*

Note: When grating or slicing lemon rind to use in any recipe, be very careful to use the outer, yellow part only. If you accidentally grate or slice off even the smallest amount of white pith that is just underneath the yellow rind, you will end up with a very bitter-tasting dish.

It was early 1988. I was now living in Gainesville, Florida. My bankroll was dwindling, as I wasn't being paid by the government any longer, so I had to try and make some money, legitimately. I

called a couple of brokers, and this one out-
fit set me up to buy a bagel luncheonette
type of place. The owner wanted $25,000 for
the place. It seated about thirty people and it
was filthy. The owner wanted out, so I spent a
couple of days casing the area and it was very
busy. The University of Florida was only a block
away. The reason the guy wanted out was because he had a larger
bagel restaurant elsewhere, and it was too much for him to handle
both. The place was worth it, but I didn't have $25,000 to lay out.

I took a shot and offered him $5,000, with the balance to be
paid at $5,000 every six months until I had it paid off. He went for
it. I cleaned it up, painted it, bought a few pictures to hang on the
walls, and so, like right away, I was in business. I kept all the
help. I didn't have to do anything but pick up the receipts every
day. At my apartment I made a chili con carne every couple of
days, and once in a while I'd make a vegetable or pea soup and
bring it in. The board of health doesn't allow you to do things like
that, but I had already taken care of one of them when I first
bought the place. I made cream puffs for the joint, too.

Those college kids loved the little restaurant. I liked the
place myself. I paid myself $600 a week and there was plenty left
over for the high rent and all the bills. Everything was going
smooth.

Then about five months later a guy walks in and says, "Hey,
bud! You're Joe Dogs, aren't you! A lot of my friends are looking
for you."

Of course I told him he was mistaken, but he seemed adamant
enough to say that he would tell an associate of his findings. He
mentioned the wise guy's name and I knew it well.

It was fortunate that I was able to sell the place the next day. I sold it for $40,000. I had asked $50,000, but I was in a hurry to get the hell away from that area. I didn't have time to bargain. The place was worth $100,000 easy. I got out of there quick.

I called there a month later and the cook, Thomas, and his lady friend, Eve, told me that a couple of shady-looking characters were there asking for me. I gave Thomas some great recipes over the phone.

Chili con Carne

1½ cups red chili beans, or 1 No. 2 can kidney beans

2 tablespoons olive oil

2 large onions, chopped

1 red bell pepper, chopped

1 pound ground beef

1 (28-ounce) can whole peeled tomatoes, chopped

1 (16-ounce) can tomato sauce (Hunt's brand preferred)

3 teaspoons tomato paste

½ teaspoon paprika

¼ teaspoon dry mustard

2 dried bay leaves

1½ tablespoons chili powder

1 teaspoon Accent

Salt to taste

Vegetable or beef stock, if needed

*S*oak beans overnight, covered, in cold water. The next day, in a saucepan, bring water to the boil and cook beans at a simmer, until soft, about 45 minutes. When done, set aside.

In a large pot, heat oil and sauté onion and pepper until limber. Add meat, broken up, and brown. Add tomatoes, tomato sauce, and paste, along with all seasonings. Simmer and stir for 2 hours. If liquid is needed, add some vegetable or beef stock. When mixture is done, stir in beans and heat thoroughly. Remove bay leaves. *Serves 6.*

Cream Puffs

SHELLS

1 cup water
¼ pound (1 stick) butter
1 cup flour, sifted
3 eggs, room temperature
Pinch salt

*I*n a saucepan, bring water to the boil and add butter. When melted, add flour all at once and stir vigorously with wooden spoon, until mixture easily leaves sides of pan and forms a ball. Add 1 egg at a time to the dough, stirring each egg into mixture until blended together smoothly.

Preheat the oven to 400°F. Grease a large cookie sheet.

Using a tablespoon and a rubber spatula, drop mixture onto sheet 1 spoonful at a time, making a swirl at top of each one. Put in freezer for 10 minutes, then bake for 40 minutes, at 400°F. Lower oven temperature to 325°F and bake shells 10 minutes more. Turn oven off and let shells sit in oven for an additional 10 minutes.

Remove puffs from oven, place them in a large brown-paper bag, and let cool. When cooled, cut a small slit in their sides. Fill a pastry bag with custard (see following recipe) or any filling of your choice, and pipe mixture into shells. *Makes about 12 shells.*

CUSTARD FILLING

> *3 egg yolks, well beaten*
> *½ cup sugar*
> *Pinch salt*
> *1 teaspoon vanilla extract*
> *2 cups milk, scalded*

*T*n a double boiler, combine beaten egg yolks, sugar, salt, and vanilla. Gradually stir in milk. Cook over low heat, stirring constantly, making sure mixture does not stick to bottom of pot. Stir until mixture coats spoon. Remove from heat, place in a glass or ceramic bowl, and cool in refrigerator. *Makes 3 cups filling.*

I had left the restaurant with about a $15,000 profit. I loaded my clothes into my car and took off. I had bought a new Cadillac Brougham while I was in the restaurant business. Now I had to worry about paying $550 a month for the car. I didn't know where to go. I rode around the west coast of Florida, trying to figure out where to make my next temporary home. I rented a well-secured apartment in Tampa. I was very apprehensive about my safety, so I had to watch where I lived. The rent was high, but $800 a month, with good security, wasn't much to pay to be safe. They wanted first and last months' rent plus security, and on top of that a $300 damage deposit. Well, there was nothing I could do. I'd asked for this type of living when I agreed to help the government fight organized crime. I stayed at that place until I no longer could afford it. I made a drastic mistake. I left myself without funds to maneuver and scheme. I left myself no alternative; I had to go to work.

I used to cook for some nice ladies once in a while at the complex where I lived, so they asked me to cook for them one more time before I left. They offered to pay me for my troubles. I told them it would be my pleasure. I asked them to pick up the groceries and said I would prepare whatever they wanted. When they told me the bill of fare, I put together a list of what I needed in the kitchen.

Blue Cheese Dressing

¾ cup mayonnaise
¼ cup buttermilk
¼ cup heavy cream
1 tablespoon lemon juice
½ teaspoon garlic, minced
⅛ teaspoon dry mustard
6 ounces blue cheese

*I*n a bowl, stir together mayonnaise, buttermilk, and cream with a wooden spoon until they are well blended. Add lemon juice, garlic, and mustard; stir well. Crumble blue cheese and stir it into dressing. Refrigerate, covered, overnight. *Makes 2 cups.*

The ladies wanted me to cook them some kind of a fancy chicken dish, so I came up with one of my own concoctions. It's a chicken-breast thing that you won't find in any recipe book. Not the name, anyway.

We'll call it:

Chicken il Formaggio

4 chicken breast halves, skinned and boned

¼ cup flour

¼ cup cornmeal

2 tablespoons butter

2 tablespoons olive oil (extra-virgin preferred)

4 slices prosciutto

4 slices Swiss cheese

¼ cup freshly grated Romano cheese

2 dried bay leaves

¼ cup chicken broth

Salt and pepper to taste

1 (16-ounce) can whole peeled tomatoes, chopped

Pound chicken with mallet or bottom of heavy skillet to ¼-inch-thick cutlets. Blend together flour and cornmeal. Dredge chicken in flour mixture, shaking off excess. In a frying pan, heat oil and butter. Sauté chicken for 2 minutes on one side, then remove from heat. With raw side of chicken facing up, layer prosciutto, Swiss cheese, and grated cheese on top. Roll up cutlets and tie middle and ends with butcher's string. Preheat the oven to 350°F.

Place chicken rolls in a baking pan or dish. Add bay leaves, chicken broth, salt, pepper, and tomatoes.

Bring mixture just to simmering on top of stove. Move to oven and bake for 30 minutes, basting occasionally with cooking liquid. When done, remove from oven, place chicken on warm platter, cut away strings, discard bay leaves, and pour sauce over all or pass separately. *Serves 4.*

With this dinner affair I prepared a pasta-with-zucchini dish.

Pasta with Zucchini

1 pound large pasta shells
1 tablespoon butter
¼ cup olive oil, divided (extra-virgin preferred)
3 cloves garlic, finely chopped
2 shallots, finely chopped
3 cups sliced zucchini
Salt and pepper to taste
3 tablespoons chopped Italian (flat-leaf) parsley

In a large stock pot, bring salted water to the boil and add pasta. Cook about 8 minutes. In a frying pan, melt butter with 2 tablespoons olive oil. Sauté garlic and shallots together until limber. Add sliced zucchini, sprinkle with salt and pepper, and sauté, turning gently to cook, about 5 to 6 minutes.

When pasta is done, drain, put back in pot, and add rest of olive oil, tossing lightly to prevent pasta from sticking. Pour zucchini sauce over pasta and toss gently while cooking together for an additional 3 to 4 minutes. Place on warm platter and sprinkle chopped parsley over the top. Serve Parmesan cheese on the side. *Serves 4.*

I left the Tampa area and moved about forty miles away. I called FBI Agent Andris Kurrins in the Brooklyn office and asked him for some help with references, as I needed them to obtain some kind of cooking job. Andy complied. I was able to land a job in a nice restaurant called Mariner, just outside of Zephyr Hills. After checking my references, the owner of the restaurant offered me $30,000 a year with benefits. I grabbed it. The chef that they had there was leaving, and he showed me around the place. He stayed with me for a week and the job was a snap. The owner was a good guy and didn't bother the kitchen help at all. Although I spotted a couple of the girls working there stealing from him, I felt it was none of my business. The job was going smooth, I was happy, my new lady friend was happy, and then once again came a phone call that made me leave the job and area in a rush.

I'd taken someone to the airport, and on the way back I'd gotten spotted and tailed to where I worked. These wise guys just would not give up. Well, for one thing, I was foolish to have stayed in the state of Florida. I kept staying within a 100-mile range of where I'd already been. You would think that it would be enough distance, but it wasn't. I'd squandered all my money. The FBI hadn't been paying me for a long time now, so I had to do something to make myself safe. I'd been dodging a lot of close calls lately. The Mob had been trying to get me ever since the time I'd been given the credit for the demise of the head Gambino boss, Paul Castellano. There seemed to be a lot more heat on me from then on.

So I had to leave my job and my new romance, a lady named

Diane. I invited Diane over to my trailer home for the last time and cooked her a bon voyage dinner. Diane brought over an Amish friendship cake, along with a starter and directions on how to continue with it.

Lobster Thermidor

2 1½-pound whole Maine lobsters, live
⅛ pound (½ stick) butter, divided
¼ cup Madeira
¼ teaspoon paprika
Pinch of nutmeg
½ teaspoon arrowroot (approximately)
2 cups heavy cream (approximately)
¼ teaspoon white pepper
Salt to taste
1 chicken bouillon cube
¼ pound baby shrimp, cleaned
½ cup sliced canned mushrooms

Kill lobsters by plunging them into a pot of boiling water and leaving there for one minute. Remove lobsters from pot and let cool. Remove meat from lobster by placing a knife just below the head, and split the shell down the spine to the end of the tail. Crack open the lobster in a butterfly fashion and discard the black intestinal vein. Remove green liver and red roe and set aside. Remove meat from tails, making sure not to break shells. With a mallet, crack the claws and remove the meat, trying not to damage it. Crack the knuckles and remove the meat. Put all meat aside and rinse the backs (shells) of the lobsters in cold water, then pat dry.

In a saucepan, melt 1 teaspoon butter until bubbly hot (do not scorch). Add the Madeira and cook until the alcohol evaporates. Add paprika, nutmeg, liver, and roe to mixture. Stir well and add arrowroot to thicken, until well blended and smooth. Add cream gradually, stirring constantly. Then add white pepper and salt to taste. Dissolve bouillon cube in 1 tablespoon of water or cream and stir into sauce mixture until well blended. Add shrimp and mushrooms, then cook over low heat for approximately 3 to 4 minutes. If necessary, add more arrowroot to thicken sauce to get desired consistency.

Put all lobster meat back into shells and broil for approximately 3 minutes, basting occasionally with remainder of butter. Put lobsters in their shells in a baking dish or pan, and spoon all Thermidor sauce over lobster meat and shells; be sure to stack the baby shrimp and mushrooms evenly in deepest front part of shells.

Bake in a preheated 400°F oven for 3 to 4 minutes, or until sauce is bubbly. Place each lobster on a plate and garnish with parsley before serving. *Serves 2.*

Amish Friendship Cake

Important!!!
- Do not use metal spoon or bowl for mixing.
- Do not refrigerate.
- If air gets in the bag, let it out.
- It is normal for batter to thicken, bubble, and ferment.

Day 1: This is the day you receive the batter. Do nothing.
Day 2: Squeeze the bag.
Day 3: Squeeze the bag.
Day 4: Squeeze the bag.
Day 5: Squeeze the bag.
Day 6: Add 1 cup flour, 1 cup sugar, and 1 cup milk and mix.
Day 7: Squeeze the bag.
Day 8: Squeeze the bag.
Day 9: Squeeze the bag.
Day 10: In a large bowl, combine 1 cup flour, 1 cup sugar, and 1 cup milk. Mix with a wooden spoon or spatula. Pour 4 1-cup starters into separate Ziploc bags. Keep one starter for yourself and give the others to friends, along with instructions.

To the remaining batter in the bowl, add:

> 1 cup oil
> 1 cup sugar
> 1 teaspoon vanilla extract
> 3 large eggs, room temperature
> 1½ teaspoons baking powder

1 large (5.25 ounces) box instant vanilla pudding
½ teaspoon salt
2 cups flour
½ cup milk
½ teaspoon baking soda
2 tablespoons cinnamon

*P*reheat the oven to 325°F.
Mix all ingredients together well. Pour batter into
2 large, well-greased and sugared loaf pans (mix in additional
cinnamon and sugar). If desired, you can add to the batter 2
cups of chopped pecans and/or ½ cup raisins. You can also
sprinkle some extra sugar mix on top. Bake for 1 hour.
Enjoy! *Serves 12.*

VARIATIONS:

Orange: 1 can mandarin oranges, drained and chopped. Use O.J.
from can instead of milk.
Peach: 1 can peaches, drained and chopped. Use juice from
peaches instead of milk.
Apple: Use chopped apples or applesauce with a little milk,
pecans, and raisins.
Lemon: Use lemon pudding instead of vanilla pudding,
a little lemon juice, and poppy seeds.
Blueberry: 1 cup blueberries and ½ cup milk.

....

Once again I was on the run. I rented a cute, clean trailer in the wooded area near Bushnell, Florida. If they found me here, they were better than the FBI. I mean, like, I was in Nowheresville, U.S.A. There was a convenience store, a small tavern-restaurant, and a post office. That was it. I had very little money, so I didn't go out anywhere. The only person I saw occasionally was FBI Agent Don Dowd from Ocala. My Cadillac had been demolished in an accident. I was without wheels, so the FBI gave me a helping hand. The New York FBI office sent funds to the Ocala office and rented a car for me to drive. I was now driving a new Pontiac Sunbird. Dowd picked me up and drove me to the Gainesville airport, where he rented the car for me. While I was there, I went to see an old flame of mine and we did the town together. That turned out to be a bad move because someone saw me and the car I was driving. The bum must have told my adversaries the latest scoop on me. However, I had a nice time on the date and went back to my trailer in the woods, which I called home.

About a week later I stopped at a gas station on I-75. I went into the adjoining coffee shop, and some lady, who appeared to be in her late thirties, walked up to me where I was seated at the counter and asked me if my name was Joe Dogs.

I said no, of course, but I must have shown apprehension in my face because she said, "Yes, it is! I know it's you! You put my father in prison and he died there because of you!"

The woman was talking really loud now, and people were staring at us. I continued to tell her she was mistaken, but it didn't do any good. I hurried out to the car and she followed, screaming obscenities at me. I quickly jumped into the automobile and left. I noticed her writing down the license plate number, but I didn't care, as it was registered in the agent's name. I drove to the trailer, extremely nervous, making all different turns, trying to make sure I wasn't being tailed.

When I got there, I called Laura Ward, the prosecutor for the Gambino trial in Brooklyn. She was sponsoring me to get into the Federal Witness Protection Program. It had been a while since she'd enrolled me for it, and I reported the coffee-shop incident to her. She said she would call headquarters and see why they were dragging their feet by not picking me up by now.

I waited and waited, but to no avail. The weeks went by, and I was still waiting to hear from the marshals. I was very apprehensive. I didn't go anywhere, except to the local convenience store to buy food.

Then one day, at about four P.M., I got up my nerve and decided to go buy some food at a supermarket. Things had been very quiet, and I was thinking that I should be picked up by the Feds any day now. So I drove out of the wooded area where I lived and got on a country road that would take me to the interstate. Approximately two miles from my trailer, I noticed a dark sedan about ten car lengths behind me. I didn't think too much of it at the time, but as a precaution, I went from forty-five mph to sixty-five mph to see if the car behind me picked up speed. It didn't, so I felt relaxed. I approached the interstate and headed southbound. I would be getting off at the very first exit that I came to, exit number 56 on Route 50. I nonchalantly looked into my rearview mirror and noticed that the car behind me was getting on also. No big deal, I thought to myself, as there were plenty of cars traveling the interstate.

I began daydreaming while driving and forgot all about the sedan. I hadn't noticed that the black car behind me was getting closer. My traveling speed was about seventy mph, and the car was inching up on me. The music I was listening to distracted my attention from the other car. I glanced in my rearview mirror and saw the sedan coming up fast. It swung over to the left lane, as if to pass me. By a mere coincidence, I happened to look in my sideview mirror and noticed two arms coming out of the front and rear right windows, with handguns. A rush of blood went to my head. I trounced on the accelerator and the Sunbird jolted and took off. (I'll say one thing about that Pontiac—it sure picked up speed fast!)

I heard a few shots ring out, one of them hitting underneath the car. I was going 110 mph as I got away from the sedan in a hurry, but the car was starting to advance on me, as the occupants were rolling pretty fast now. I became panic-stricken and started to shake. My whole life was flashing before my eyes. I started to pray. Please, God! Save me from these terrible people, and I'll go to church every Sunday. Two more shots! One of them hit something on a rear wheel. We started going down a slight grade and their car was almost at my level. I was leaning to my right, shaking like hell. Then I sat up and hit the brakes as hard and fast as I could, leaning over to the passenger's side once again. The little Sunbird screeched sideways and swerved to the right on the embankment. I heard a barrage of shots as the sedan flew by me. Some of the bullets hit the car frame underneath me—I heard the clang twice.

When my car came to a halt, I was lying on the seat on the passenger's side all crumbled up. I was trembling and I could feel pressure like someone was stepping on my chest, and my left arm was heavy with pain. I was having a hard time breathing as I tried to lift myself up to see if the black sedan was stopped or coming back, and I was still gasping for air when a man put a nitroglycerin tablet under my tongue.

When I sat up I was still trembling. I noticed there were five cars that had stopped and witnessed the whole incident—one lady said that the bullets had been ricocheting off the pavement. Ten minutes had gone by, and I was still in shock. I was trying to talk, but the words wouldn't come out. Someone had put in a call to the police, who still hadn't arrived, and I was thinking: Where are the cops when I need them? I decided to leave, so I mustered up my strength and thanked the people who'd shown concern for me and allowed that I would be all right. A couple of them said I should wait and report what happened to the police, so I said I'd head for the police station right away. I was in the car, with my eyes still filled with tears of fright.

I started the Pontiac up and took off. There was a bridge about a quarter of a mile down the interstate. I passed underneath it and turned left to go north. I headed north to Route 50 and got off the interstate. Taking care, I got back to my trailer two hours later.

I called Agent Dowd and told him of the botched attempt to kill me. Dowd offered to let me stay at his residence for safety, but I declined. I called Laura Ward the next morning at the Brooklyn Task Force and she made sure that the marshals picked me up pronto.

I met my first marshal in Daytona Beach, Florida, that morning, and he handed me $500 and said it was "walking-around money." He put me on a plane to somewhere near the end of the world, and as I sat on the plane with tears in my eyes, I could remember the words of Tommy "T.A." Agro: "Hey, Joey! Let me tell you something, my friend! If I don't get you, my *famiglia* will! You better watch your back the rest of your f____ life, because I'll bury you! I won't miss you next time, and I'll take this promise with me to the grave!"

It's more than twelve years since Tommy Agro died. I'm still running and looking over my shoulder. He's definitely keeping his word!

After bouncing around from state to state, city to city, one hotel to another for sixteen weeks, with the marshals, of course, I finally settled down in Memphis, Tennessee. When I got off the plane, the marshal who picked me up said, "Joe Dogs! It's good to meet you! I hear you're a very good cook! After you're settled, how about cooking something up and we'll chow down."

Naturally, I complied.

After I got settled in an apartment with new furniture and all the other things I needed, and with the money the government gave me, the marshal came over and asked, "Well, Joe, what are you going to cook?"

"I think I'm going to make a nice new Italian dish," I said. "I recently got the recipe from a chef who just got off the boat from Italy. It's called . . . Hey, wait a minute! Fuhgedaboudit! That's another cookbook!"

Acknowledgments for "Cooking on the Lam"

Marrone! Fuhgedaboudit! Another cookbook. I must be intelligent. Maybe even smart. Although without these wonderful people in mention, this project would not be completed.

My thanks go out to my two close friends, Tommy Ray and Charlie Howard, for their support literally, and for their encouragement for me to continue writing. Also to my good friend R. D. Walker, thank you for all your time and the use of your computer. More thanks and congratulations to Matt and his lovely wife, Felicia. I'd also like to thank Greg and his extremely sexy, beautiful wife Sara, whom I've had many dreams about. I'd like to express my gratitude to my cuz Lou and his lovely fiancée, Rhonda, for the use of their kitchen whenever I wanted to perfect one of my culinary delights. Also, thank you, Carolyn Beauchamp, my pretty actress friend, for your contribution. Also I send my best to a good friend, David Wright, and his darling sister Karen from Atlanta, Georgia. Many thank-yous go to some of the staff at Simon & Schuster—Carol Bowie, Nancy Inglis, Jonathon Brodman, and Jim Stoller—for their help on the editing and corrections.

Being away from my native town, New York City, I naturally had to make new friends, so I would like to make mention of a few

lovelies that helped me suppress my loneliness. There's the beautiful Sandra with her sensuous lips. Then there's the very pretty "blond" Julie, who is the only lady that I know of that makes a chicken salad sandwich from a can of Chicken of the Sea. But what a doll she is. Then there's also Norma, the cute chick with a tough little body. I must mention these two hot-looking chicks that have been exceptionally nice to me, Charla and Kelly. Thanks to Ginny and Bill for their patience with me when I needed something typed. Thanks a million for all your friendships.

I'd like to thank all the guys in town that know of me and accepted me as their friend: Wiley; Ron; Jonathan and his wife, Debbie; Bobbie; Moe; Tracy Woods (no relation to Tiger); Robert and his wife, Tracie; Glenn; David and his wife, Annie. Also to René and Al; remember the Alamo! Last but not least, thanks to Lance and his beautiful wife, Robin, who together look like they both stepped out of *Vogue* magazine. Thank you all for your friendship.

I would be remiss if I didn't mention Melanie, whom I cherish. Thank you, darling, for the treasured moments we spent together. I'll never forget you, Dear Heart!

About the Author

JOSEPH "JOE DOGS" IANNUZZI was a mobster with the Gambino crime family before teaming up with a deep-cover FBI informant and appearing as a star witness at five major Mob trials. The author of *Joe Dogs: The Life and Crimes of a Mobster*, he entered the Witness Protection Program after testifying.

Printed in the United States
By Bookmasters